God Is in the Bedroom Too

P. B. WILSON

HARVEST HOUSE PUBLISHERS

EUGENE, OREGON

D1310164

Cover design by Koechel Peterson, Minneapolis, Minnesota

GOD IS IN THE BEDROOM TOO
Copyright © 2002 by P.B. Wilson
Published by Harvest House Publishers
Eugene, Oregon 97402

Library of Congress Cataloging-in-Publication Data
Wilson, P. B. (P. Bunny), 1950-
    God is in the bedroom too/ P. B. Wilson.
        p. cm.
    ISBN 0-7369-0796-3 (pbk.)
        1.Wives—Religious life. 2. Christian women—Religious life. 3.
        Sex—Religious aspects—Christianity. I. Title.
BV4528.15 .W55 2002
241' .66—dc21   2002003155

Printed in the United States of America.

    03 04 05 06 07 08 09 10 11 / VP-KB / 10 9 8 7 6 5 4 3

*To my children and future generations—
may you walk in God's
sexual freedom.*

Acknowledgments

I would like to thank my hero, Frank. We've been walking together since 1973 and have weathered the storms of life. This book would not have been possible if you had not reached out to where I was and brought me to where I needed and wanted to be. Your loyalty, commitment, and faithfulness have inspired me to reach higher and jump farther than I ever imagined. I honor and salute you, my beloved.

To my publisher, Harvest House. Your support and commitment to excellence has impacted the world and has provided an outlet for me to share my book. Thank you for believing in me. To my editor, Lela Gilbert, who refuses to settle for less than the best. You are awesome!

To my dear friend, Mary Dumas. Thank you for lunch at the Tea Rose Garden and for wanting to read my book line by line (twice). Your input was invaluable. To Sandy Snavely, thank you for the gift wrap and the bows. I value our friendship. And to Kodua Michelle, thank you for holding my arms up at the last hour. You too read my book twice and offered valuable insight. Your words of encouragement are indelibly etched in my heart.

Thank you to all those who gave me their input as I moved through this project. In alphabetical order: Azzure, Christy, Courtney, Desiree, Elenor, Fawn, Harry, Jason, Launi, Leah, Marilyn, Melanie, Peggy, Susan, and Varetta. I appreciate you.

Contents

There is a cross hanging in the hallway to the right of our bedroom door. It's not there because of some religious tradition. It is not a souvenir from a foreign land. And no, it isn't there to ward off demons.

The cross is a reminder. Even before we enter our bedroom, it helps us remember God is always present. He is aware of all we say and do. When we walk into that private room, our relatives, friends, business associates, and church members are nowhere to be found. We are in our secret haven, a place reserved for us in which we are refreshed, rekindled, and romanced.

The cross reminds us that God is the giver of every good and perfect gift. And one of His greatest gifts to us is the relationship we share with each other as man and wife.

1

Don't Settle for Anything Less Than...

~

*I*s this a book about sex? Yes, but even more so, it is a book about spiritual maturity. That is why I have chosen to include comments to single people as well. Throughout this book, there will be "single moments," indicated by the title *Especially for Singles*. At those times, I will be speaking to the single woman, although many statements will apply to single men as well.

My attention is focused primarily on married women. But since godly sex involves both wives and their husbands, some wives will want to share the learned principles in this book with their spouses. I have made that a little easier by summing up the book for married men in chapter 10. In that chapter, my husband, Frank, has written a special section just for men.

And because parents have a responsibility to communicate God's ways to their children, I have written a special section for teenagers in chapter 11. The last chapter has been designed so it can be removed and given to a teenager. I have found that many parents teach teenagers about their body parts but often fail to share in-depth conversations about sex. And yet, their youngsters are constantly confronted with sexual comments, information, and innuendos through various school conversations and media and printed materials. They don't have to go looking for it because it comes to them. I have been careful not to arouse their passions, although I am forthcoming with important information.

Why am I so concerned about the subject of godly sexuality? For one thing, Frank and I have counseled hundreds of men and women—married, single, and divorced—and we have learned how little these people have been told about such a key subject. In fact for years, I was confused concerning the subject of sex myself. I knew I loved my husband, but my level of sexual satisfaction made me doubt my ability to give and receive love. I thought sex would be much more enjoyable than it actually was (I definitely don't feel that way anymore) and was at a loss about whom I could talk to concerning my dilemma. God's Word, the Bible, provided both necessary instructions and beautiful secrets for me, along with some other resources as well. Now I am delighted to share with you what I've learned.

Games

The game was fun and entertaining. Sitting across from me was one of my daughters, who was nine years old at the time. It was her turn for the one-night retreat I enjoy annually with each of our girls. She and I checked into a hotel and were now sitting cross-legged on the bed playing with words. She searched the letters on her game board and then shouted, "I have a word!" Her smile, however, quickly turned to a look of concern and she hastily added, "No, I don't."

"Let me see," I said.

She responded, "No, it's okay. I'll find another one."

"Come on," I nudged.

"You'll get mad."

"No, I won't."

Slowly, she turned her letters around, and with flushed cheeks she revealed the source of her embarrassment. With three little letters she spelled out an important message: It was time for me to set her foundation on how she viewed the subject of *s-e-x*. It was also clear that I needed to move from teaching her the parts of the body to having more open conversations about when and who and why and what for. Obviously, she was beginning to hear comments, explanations, and opinions from her schoolmates. I knew too well what she heard at school would fall far short of God's truth. It was my responsibility to teach her that truth not only through what was spoken but also in my demonstration of a healthy attitude toward my own womanly sexuality. There would be time for me to say more later. That moment simply called for an appropriate response.

As she searched my face for a reaction, I announced, "That's a good word! Sex was created by God and that makes it wonderful."

This sensitive child seemed to sigh with relief, and we returned to our game. Her concerned expression was now replaced by a smile. I stored that moment away in my heart, knowing it was just the first baby step that we would take together along her path into womanhood.

> *For years, I was confused concerning the subject of sex. God's Word, the Bible, provided the necessary instruction for me.*

How Well We Remember

Perhaps you don't have children, or maybe your sons and daughters are now adults themselves. But one thing is sure; you were once a child yourself. And when we reflect back on childhood, it's easy to see, both consciously and unconsciously, that we absorbed the viewpoint our parents or guardians held concerning sex. We saw their attitude written upon their faces, and we heard it in their voices anytime the topic surfaced.

Do you remember, when statements were made about the subject, whether your parents' response was short, abrupt, or unpleasant? Perhaps your mother referred to sexual intercourse as a duty; maybe your father cleared his throat and looked the other way. You may have heard remarks like, "Nice girls don't do that," or "Just keep your skirt down until you get married." It may well be that these throwaway lines were supposed to be enough information to keep you pure until you reached your wedding day.

Fortunately, there's more to the story than that. God Himself has given us principles and strategies that can keep a single person from sexual sin, while liberating the married couple to enjoy what He has prepared for them. These can be summed up in the statement, "Don't settle for anything less than saved sex!"

Saved sex is more glorious than anything the world has to offer. It is designed to be enjoyed by a Christian man and woman joined together by God in holy matrimony. However, being a Christian does not guarantee sexual satisfaction. An enjoyable and fulfilling marital relationship also requires an understanding of God's intention and purpose for the couple's sexual relationship.

It's interesting that sex is the only thing in the Bible that is sinful when we are single and holy when we are married. Sexual intercourse is commissioned and blessed by God Himself. So precious is the experience that singles should take notice that they will be ripped off if they participate in it prior to their wedding night.

As I told my daughter that night, "Sex was created by God and that makes it wonderful." It is a celebration of God's creation, and He is pleased when we desire the one we love within the confines of marriage. Since He designed sex, doesn't it stand to reason that He would be delighted when we practice it according to His will? Sex as God created it results in satisfaction for both partners. To violate the principle of saved sex is a lonely and unfulfilled experience. It subtracts God from the equation and leads to a desolate place. Each encounter diminishes the possibility of a blessed sexual plateau ever being reached.

Saved sex begins with recognizing that, yes, God is in the bedroom. We know that He is in all places, at all times, even during our most private moments. What goes on between a married couple is sacred and holy and the marriage bed is "undefiled" (Hebrews 13:4 NKJV). It is sobering to acknowledge that God is present there. But it is also refreshing to know that we are experiencing something He created for our procreation and pleasure. This knowledge directs and controls our interaction with one another.

In the book of Genesis, God brings Adam and Eve together. The Lord made the man and shaped the woman. Then, He presented her to Adam, and boy was Adam glad! It's important to note that Genesis 2:25 says, "The man and his wife were both naked, and they felt no shame." They were free to see each other in the deepest intimacy without embarrassment, guilt, or fear.

It was sin that caused Adam and Eve to cover their bodies and hide their faces. From the moment they failed to obey God, nakedness became something to be hidden, revealed only in darkened rooms or in the shadows of our minds. Nudity was transformed into the devil's workshop where distortions were created and secrets were hatched.

"Stolen water is sweet" (Proverbs 9:17), became the devil's theme song. Perhaps we don't recognize the melody immediately because he hums it ever so softly, but before we know it, we too may be humming along, oblivious to the words of the song. This isn't the way it should be. In reality, God has redeemed the human body along with everything else about His creation. Within the proper boundaries, there is nothing shameful about our unveiled bodies. Because of Christ's redemptive grace, married men and women can stop feeling ashamed, and they can do so by no longer being, "conformed to this world but be transformed by the renewing of your mind" (Romans 12:2 NKJV).

When we embrace the concept of saved sex, it frees us up to completely enjoy something God created for procreation, recreation, and communication. It also liberates us to stand in amazement that He loved us enough to give such a wonderful and precious gift. Saved sex allows us to understand we have been forgiven of all past, repented mistakes and can walk in a glorious freedom designed only for His children. Saved sex liberates us to enjoy marriage to its fullest extent.

> *Don't settle for anything less than saved sex!*

Especially for Singles

Maybe you're a single woman and feeling a little left out of the discussion. You're not left out at all. Saved sex equips you to abstain from unholy entanglements and to live your life wholly and completely devoted to God. Coming into the knowledge of how it works will heighten your determination to experience nothing less than saved sex. You will view sexual temptations through a new set of eyes. Enticements that once would have stimulated you to fall into sin will become distasteful from the onset. Once you've committed yourself to saved sex, you will be equipped to take the road that leads to God's throne of grace. Understanding saved sex *before marriage* prepares you for a fulfilling sex life *after marriage*.

A Worldly School of Thought

"Greetings. Come right in to the Modern World's Academy of Sexual Pleasure. Singles and married couples, you are equally welcome. My name is Dr. D, and there is room for everyone, but please be patient while standing in the long lines. As you make your way to the front door, notice that we've gone to great lengths to beautify the building. Isn't the landscaping fabulous? A great deal of thought went into constructing something that would be functional yet pleasing to the eye."

With hopes high and fantasies intact, prospective students wait eagerly to enroll and learn all they can. As they read through the list of courses offered and study the class descriptions, their hearts pound with excitement about all they will be learning. The list goes on and on but following are a few highlights:

- It's your body, and you can do whatever you like with it as long as you're not hurting anyone.

- Sex is designed to satisfy an individual personally and how that is accomplished is each person's choice.

- Having sex before marriage won't affect you after you are married.

- Whether you are a teenager or adult, there is nothing wrong with satisfying yourself; the act of masturbation eliminates unwanted pregnancies, relieves stress, and brings a sweet release.

- If you are a female participant, should you conceive during sex, then abortion is a viable solution.

- If you are a teenage boy, you are free to "sow your wild oats" so you can get your sex drive out of your system and settle down later on.

≈ • ≈ • ≈

There is certainly another way of looking at sexuality, but you won't find it in the Modern World's Academy of

Sexual Pleasure. My daughter Christy attends a university in New York. As a new freshman, she was excited and was looking forward to the dormitory experience. Not long after she moved in, she called home and said, "Mom, I was walking down the hallway of my dorm and you'll never guess what I saw. Someone hung a poster on their door that says, 'It's not premarital sex if you don't plan to get married!'"

Christy laughed and continued, "At first I thought about how much sense that made, but as I kept walking I thought, 'Hey, wait a minute. That's wrong!' Mom, it seemed to be such a logical statement! You know, if a Christian person doesn't know the Bible and the truth about sex, I can see how easily they could be misled by such a cunning lie."

Consequences of Unsaved Sex

I knew when she left home the world would soon be trying to instruct Christy on the subject of sex. Therefore, one day I chose to put my thoughts on paper and urged her to consider the consequences of premarital sex. The list is as follows:

1. It will break God's heart.

2. Sin will enter the relationship and negatively alter it.

3. The man will lose respect for the woman (usually unspoken) no matter what he says.

4. God created man to be the pursuer. Once a woman has been conquered, an element of fun and excitement leaves the relationship.

5. You'll lose your "specialness" (even though he'll swear differently).

6. There'll be nothing to look forward to on your wedding night.

7. Once you start down that road, what will be your reason for stopping? Use that reasoning now.

8. Sexual activity will come to be expected.

9. Pregnancy is very possible.

10. Guilt will enter the relationship.

11. Self-control will be destroyed. You will need this in your marriage to ward off behaviors like rage, lust, and adultery.

12. Your Christian testimony will be tainted.

13. Your younger sister is following in your footsteps. Is this what you would want for her?

14. You'll lose your testimony with your children. What will you tell them when they reach their teenage years and ask what you did when you were young?

15. You'll weaken your potential husband's walk in Christ, and he'll be your spiritual leader one day.

Perhaps you've "been there, done that" and nodded your head at each point. Isn't it amazing how these truths apply? The consequences are inevitable. Hopefully, the above information coupled with your desire to participate only in saved sex will help you stay sexually pure.

One of the greatest deceptions I have ever witnessed was broadcast on television not long ago. It was an interview with an ex-priest who is now a director of sexually explicit films. These films are being distributed and accepted by certain churches. This misguided director explained that many married couples have sexual problems, and they can find solutions by watching his movies. He went on to say the people participating in the X-rated scenes were married couples who "love each other" and had made themselves available to teach different sexual techniques. Shaking my head, I thought about something my pastor sometimes says, "You can count on Satan to be three things: logical, rational, and *wrong.*"

What one married couple does sexually has nothing to do with any other couple. Every person's body is unique, and what satisfies one may not satisfy another. Saved sex is devoted to exploring and discovering what pleases *our* spouse, not someone else's spouse. We'll talk more about this later.

For now, let's return to the Modern World's Academy of Sexual Pleasure. It is teaching sex without shame but neglecting to mention that guilt is a required subject. Dr. D's name is short for Deception. He would never mention "soul ties" that are formed between sexual partners.* Nor would Dr. D reveal the deep regret that follows each participant through the halls of time. In his school of thought, Wisdom is not part of the curriculum, and sex becomes one huge playground.

It is interesting that both sexes, after joining the fraternity and sorority of the sexually active, try to encourage as many others as possible to become a card-carrying member of the club. And information about club activities is as close as the click of a computer mouse. Chat rooms focusing on sex are innumerable, allowing people to participate in pornographic discussions, and the Internet is loaded with pictures. They can be conveniently accessed by our youth, and many are being led into sexual activity through these channels.

The world's school has some dark, hidden classes, with teachers who attempt to enroll students in their curriculum

---

* The emotions and will live in the soul. I believe that when you have sex, your soul is connected to your sexual partner's. Unconsciously, a piece of you remains with the other person, and the tie needs to be broken through repentance and acceptance of God's forgiveness.

as early as possible, with or without their consent. Incest and molestation warp the thinking of children and come close to destroying the abused child's ability to experience a holy, satisfying sexual experience as an adult. Child molesters are perverted and driven by lust. Any adult who has come through such a damaging experience would seem to have no hope. Thankfully for them, when God's redemption enters their lives, and the principle of saved sex enters the picture, everything changes.

Rape is another vicious act that robs its victims of self-respect and dignity. This crime is permanently etched in the memory of raped individuals, and only a miracle can deliver them from the haunting images of the assault. Again the concept of saved sex changes everything. Once the lines that have been drawn by a cruel artist are erased, a masterpiece is revealed. The hand that paints that masterpiece can erase not only the effects of what has been done to victims, but also the harm that men and women have done to themselves.

> *The world's school teaches sex without shame but neglects to mention that guilt is a required subject.*

In days gone by, you may have led a loose, promiscuous lifestyle. Perhaps your sexual partners have been too numerous to count. But have you ever had *saved sex?* If not, then you have something to look forward to, something you've never experienced before. It will truly be your "first time." What has been stripped or robbed from your life through misinformation, violation, or lust can be replaced with a fresh start. You'll enroll in a new school and your teacher, the Holy Spirit, will instruct you on God's original intentions about sex. You'll find the teaching to be most interesting, informative, and fun!

The Second School of Thought

"Welcome to God's School of *Saved Sex.* My name is Holiness, and I will be your tour guide. Singles, you are the only one in your classroom, and couples, we have a classroom just for the two of you. Every person here will be taught on a very personal basis. The curriculum has been designed to meet your individual and collective needs. As stated in John 14:26, the Holy Spirit will be your teacher. There is a lot to be learned and, I might add, a lot to be *unlearned.*"

In God's school, the first lesson teaches the basics. It starts with the fact that sex is created and ordained by God. If its only purpose was procreation, that could have been accomplished in many ways: holding hands, looking deeply in each other's eyes, or having a stork drop a baby on our doorstep. God didn't need sex to create Adam and Eve; He just made them. And He could go right on creating new people if He wanted to. So, even though sex is used as a conduit for reproduction, it has a broader purpose in God's mind.

The second lesson is a required course you'll need to take—if you don't know about male and female body parts and how they function, you should. And one of the best sources for this information is found in a book written by Dr. Ed Wheat entitled *Intended for Pleasure.* It is thorough and walks the reader through the intricate design of the body and what takes place physiologically in order for the male and female to participate in sex. When you discover how intricate and complex the sexual act is, you'll be utterly amazed. You'll walk away thanking God for His design. When I gained the knowledge of what is actually taking place before, during, and after sex, I was overwhelmed by the marvel of God's creation.

The third lesson gives instruction on what to expect in the sex act itself. It opens the married person's eyes to an experience that is able to fulfill and edify. Doubt, fear, or guilt cannot accompany saved sex. Even if only one person in the marriage is willing to seek the information, the other spouse will be profoundly affected by it.

Besides the lessons I've mentioned, I think you're going to discover that you will want to wait to have sex only after marriage. And if you've been in violation of that principle, the steps to correct the situation will be provided. In this school, principles of sexual godliness are taught in such a way that even a young man or woman can understand them.

The knowledge of what transpires if we violate God's will for our sexual purity will further reinforce a single person's decision to wait until after marriage to have sex. The slogan "I won't settle for anything less than saved sex!" will soon be stamped on your psyche. That determination will guide your footsteps, your thought life, and your body down a path of newfound freedom.

Lastly, we will explore the strengthening of our relationship with God that takes place when we understand and apply His sexual principles to our lives. We'll reflect upon His intent and purpose for sexual intercourse so that it brings freedom not only to us, but also to those around us. Our testimony will shine as a bright light. It will serve as salt to the listener, creating a thirst for the truth.

> "...sex is created and ordained by God."

The lessons at God's School of Saved Sex are taught layer upon layer, precept upon precept, and graduation day is exciting! The single person receives a diploma with the determination to stay pure until God sends them their spouse. They will be equipped to remain strong through even the greatest of temptations. And married couples will enter into the joy that awaits them during physical intimacy with one another.

A Good Understanding

Every Christian is called to walk in truth (John 8:32). Why should it seem strange that this includes sexual truth? We've been held in the grip of lies, deceit, and misinformation for too long. Unfortunately, a good number of believers did not know about God's School of Saved Sex, and they have failed miserably in that aspect of life. But with the Bible as our instruction manual, it's never too late. We can always claim the ability to walk in sexual freedom.

I have a personal interest in this subject because I was among those who failed in the earlier part of my life. My experience reminds me of an incident that happened recently. After entering my optometrist's office, I decided to use the ladies' restroom before my name was called. As I walked into the bathroom, I noticed that a girl about eight years old was washing her hands. After I closed the stall door and put down the items I had in my arms, something startling happened. The lights went out!

Immediately I called out, but there was no answer. My first thought was that the little girl had flicked off the light switch on her way out. That wasn't too alarming, but because there were no windows, it was very, very dark. I couldn't even see my hand held up directly in front of me. Then another, scarier thought came to mind. What if it wasn't the little girl who had turned the lights off? What if someone with ill intent had come in as she was leaving, had seen what stall I had entered, and was now waiting just outside my door?

Fear and confusion began to surge within me. I could feel my heart pounding against my chest. What was I to do? If I decided to wait until someone else came in to use the bathroom and turned the light back on, I might be stuck in there for a very long time since there were only a few people in the office. On the other hand, if I decided to leave the stall, there was no telling what awaited me immediately outside. Nonetheless, I had to make a decision. I determined to take my chances and open the door.

Reaching for the lock on the door, I realized I hadn't paid any attention to how it operated. Should I slide it, lift it, or turn it? Did it move to the right or the left? Taking some deep breaths, I fumbled with the lock and finally the door opened. As I took one step forward, I waited to hear or feel if there was someone else present. That was difficult, considering my rapid breathing and the sound of my heart beating in my ears. I tried to remember the configuration of the room. Did I enter from the right or the left? How far did I walk to the stall? Everything was a blur.

I took two more small steps and stopped. Then I did something I should have done at the very beginning. I prayed, "Father, help me!" As peace began to slowly cover me, a thought arose. If I stood very still, perhaps I could hear voices from the lobby area and I would know which way to turn. I strained to listen. Finally, to my left, someone coughed. I took one step forward, turned to my left, and as I looked down there was a sliver of light shining beneath the bathroom door. Slowly I inched my way forward until I found my way out.

This incident is a pretty good example of how some of us have to find our way in the dark as far as sexual information is concerned. As a teenager, I was taught very little about the subject, and what was said was not positive. Predictably, I launched out on my own, experimenting along the way. And what I found was unfulfilling and empty. When I married at age 22, I thought everything would be different. My husband was a Christian, and we waited until after holy matrimony to have sex. But, to my dismay, it was as if someone had turned off the light. I felt completely disoriented and unsatisfied, and I didn't know who to talk to.

I remained in darkness for five years, convinced that I was the problem and there was no help for me. But one day I turned and saw the sliver of light, helping me find my way. It turned out the information I so desperately needed was contained in my Bible. In the days that followed, I studied God's Word with new eyes, as well as reading other written material about how God designed our bodies sexually. What I learned released me to enjoy God's creation. It changed my life and my marriage. Now I'm excited about sharing what I learned with you.

Perhaps you also feel as if you're standing in an unlit room with confusion all around. If you will be still (Psalm 46:10), you will hear God gently calling you. As you turn toward His truth, the light under the door of your life will lead you to the truth. But the Lord will not be the only one beckoning you; I'll be there too. Sharing my journey to sexual freedom will be my delight. Isn't it wonderful to know that we serve a God who cares about every aspect of our lives? This is going to be fun! Welcome to *God's School of Saved Sex*.

> *W*alking in truth is a calling upon every Christian's life (John 8:32). For many, it may seem strange that this includes sexual truth.

2

A Secret Haven

~

The newly married couple had just parted lips after a kiss at the altar. They were finally Mr. and Mrs. The two of them wanted to dash for the car and ride off into the sunset. But there were pictures to take, hands to shake, and a reception to navigate through. Even though they went through the motions, their hearts and minds were longing for their *secret haven*—that secluded retreat where the two of them would feast on their freshly committed love.

Millions of times a year, all over the world, men and women are pronounced man and wife. The sizes and details of the weddings vary, but the result is the same. They are henceforth joined in holy matrimony. What happens next, however, can either lift their spirits to the skies or shatter their dreams. I'm talking about what takes place after the guests leave and the couple is alone. As everyone knows, the next stage of their life together is called the *honeymoon*.

Now a honeymoon is supposed to be nothing short of sheer bliss. Yet I've heard an incredible number of stories relating the disappointment experienced by the husband, the wife, or both. In many cases, the lack of fulfillment was a result of their having violated the secret haven prior to

> *Even though they went through the motions, their hearts and minds were longing for their secret haven.*

marriage by participating in inappropriate sexual contact. But even when a couple has saved themselves for their wedding night, satisfaction is not always guaranteed. Why? Because unless they started their sexual relationship with an accurate vision of what to expect, the honeymooners are probably going to be disappointed.

A Trio of Honeymoon Stories

"Bill and Jan" knew each other in high school. But it wasn't until they were sophomores in college and joined the choir that sparks began to fly. Their college chorus traveled to other schools and events throughout the year, and sometimes that involved lengthy bus trips. On one particular occasion the two ended up sitting next to each other and the rest is history. They talked all the way to their destination and back, and from that day on, they were inseparable.

Marriage was a given for Bill and Jan. It wasn't a matter of *if* they were going to get married but *when*. In Bill's junior year he was able to purchase a car, and that was when the great temptation began. After almost every date, Bill and Jan ended up parked in a dark spot, and it wasn't long until the windows were getting steamed up. Jan was committed to keeping herself pure until marriage, and Bill wanted to honor her commitment, but he didn't see anything wrong with what he described as "a little fooling around." After all, Jan was the only woman for him. He would never want to marry and spend the rest of his life with anyone else. So why not? As time went by, their car encounters became more and more exploratory. Before long, each occasion left Jan racked with guilt.

On their wedding day, Jan was relieved when she walked down the aisle. She and Bill had done a lot of things, but somehow they'd managed not to go "all the way." That night, when they were finally alone in their hotel room, the kissing began, and it couldn't help but remind Jan of their many parked-car adventures. It was like old times, and Jan didn't like that at all. They had just gotten married. This was supposed to be new! Instead, it just seemed like more of the same. Bill and Jan consummated their marriage, but Jan was left with emptiness in her soul. When I talked to her for the first time, after she and Bill had been married for 15 years, Jan was still feeling the same way.

Then there was Donald and Joyce. It was love at first sight when they met at church. Their pastor had strict dating rules, and they mostly saw each other at group activities. When it was very clear that they wanted to be a couple, they met with the pastor and faithfully followed the dating program outlined by the church. After completing premarital counseling, they set the wedding date. Their first kiss was exchanged at the altar, after they had said their vows. The whole church was blessed by the way the two of them had conducted their courtship.

Donald was a fairly new Christian when he met Joyce. He was the product of a broken home, and he had split his time between his parents as he was growing up. His mother had always attended church regularly, but his father loved to party and get drunk. Donald was 13 years old when he found girlie magazines under his father's bed. Every month a new one was added to the collection, and the boy waited for it anxiously because he loved looking at the pictures. As he grew older, he also began reading the stories that came with each issue. When he became an adult, he began acquiring the magazines on his own.

Donald also developed a taste for pornographic videos, and consequently he spent a lot of time fantasizing about sex. Fortunately, that all changed when he became a Christian. He burned his magazines and threw out his videos. It was very difficult, however, to get the images out of his mind. He fought them with all his might.

On his wedding night, Donald's fantasies of times past came rushing back. Now he was with his wife, the woman he loved, and Joyce would fulfill his desires. Unfortunately, Donald was so driven by his sexual cravings, and the mental images that fueled them, he took little thought for Joyce's pleasure. And in the process, in her eyes her new husband became a different person. His lustful words and aggressive actions seemed to come from someone else, someone she didn't know.

Joyce cried herself to sleep. Donald stayed awake all night hating himself for what he had done. There was no way he was going to tell Joyce about the magazines and videos that had cluttered his past, because he was sure she would think he was an awful person. He would just try harder the next time to be more considerate.

Nonetheless, the damage had been done. Joyce felt violated, and her dreams of a gentle and caring honeymoon were destroyed forever. The hardest part, however, was when she returned home and looked into what seemed like a million faces that all asked the same question, "So how was your honeymoon?" She smiled each time and said, "Oh, it was great!" But with each question came the reminder of her great disappointment.

Especially for Singles

God has a good reason for wanting you to abstain from sexual activity of every kind until you are married. His Word also instructs you to keep your mind clean and pure. As Donald and Joyce found out the hard way, those directions come into clear focus once you are married and enter your secret haven.

There are countless stories, but I'll share one more. David and Shirley both had their share of premarital sex with a number of different people prior to meeting. David will never forget the day he saw Shirley for the first time. It was a warm Sunday morning when David pulled into a gas station. A good-looking woman was pumping gas at the island ahead of him, and her blue dress and high heels caught his eye. Everyone else around him was attired for a relaxing afternoon at the beach or a picnic. Not this lady.

As David walked past Shirley, he stated, "I'd sure hate for you to get that pretty dress all dirty. Would you like me to pump that gas for you?"

When Shirley looked up at him with her bright smile, he was immediately captured. She looked at David with what he still calls her "happy eyes" and replied, "No, but thank you for asking."

David walked to the gas station attendant and paid for his gas. On his way back to his car, Shirley was just putting the gas nozzle back in its place. He knew that he couldn't just let her drive away not knowing whether he would see her again. Hesitantly, he approached Shirley and said, "I don't mean to offend you, but is there any way I might be able to see you again?"

With one fluid motion, Shirley reached for her purse and scribbled something on a piece of paper. "Sure," she responded.

After she drove away, David looked down at the note and realized that she had written the name and address of a church on the torn piece of notebook paper. David chuckled and whispered under his breath, "Well, I guess we won't be seeing each other after all."

A month passed. David could not get Shirley out of his mind. He had been with a lot of women, but something about her was different. When he walked into the church, it seemed as if every head turned to look at him. David searched the pews for Shirley and spotted her in the second row. There was no way he was going to sit that close to the preacher, so he sat in the back of the church. He had to admit that the service was quite moving and the words of the sermon touched him deeply. At first David had shown up simply to win Shirley's affections. But after that sermon, he found himself wanting to go to hear more about God's Word.

It took two months, but finally David convinced Shirley to have lunch with him after church. She utterly intrigued him. Towards the end of their meal, Shirley looked squarely at David and said, "There is something you need to know about me. My desire is to be married and have children one day. If that isn't your goal, then I'd appreciate it if you would not pursue me."

David started to reply, but before he could say anything, Shirley added, "Also, I need to tell you something else. I will only be intimately involved with my future husband. I wish I could say he'll be the first. I can't say that. But I've been keeping myself pure for five years and I am committed to doing so until I am married."

There was a long uncomfortable pause and then David responded, "No woman has ever said that to me. Do you mind if I think about it?"

"No, I don't mind at all. You just need to understand that my mind is made up."

Getting Shirley to go out with him was one of David's greatest challenges. Continuing to date her according to her standards was an even greater one. Usually within three dates he would have been sleeping with any woman he dated. And if the truth be told, before Shirley turned her life over to the Lord, she had been doing the same thing with men. It was difficult for those two to abstain but they succeeded. It wasn't long before Shirley and David finally got married.

The real struggle for Shirley began on their honeymoon, where she found herself comparing David with her past lovers. She almost slipped at one point and called him by someone else's name. Expressions and phrases said to other men were now being said to David, and she hated the way it made her feel. David, too, was faced with some unwelcome memories and uninvited flashbacks. Still, in the midst of their recollections and regrets, the two of them were grateful for the purity they had chosen to maintain. And when they prayed together, they thanked God for His willingness to give them a new beginning based on His forgiveness and cleansing.

≈ • ≈ • ≈

There is a common thread that runs through these three stories. Each couple was, at some point, unaware of God's design of physical intimacy in marriage. And each of them had to deal with the consequences of past behavior, even though God ultimately blessed their marriages and helped them to work through the challenges brought about by the past.

Abstaining from sex in singleness blesses the marriage with self-control, obedience, and humility. Clearly, however, it does not provide the information necessary for married couples to enjoy a satisfying sexual experience. And those who have participated in premarital sex need to understand the importance of repentance, receiving forgiveness, and forgiving themselves. Then, they too, need to appropriate God's plan for physical intimacy in their secret haven.

The secret haven is an area set aside for a married couple to experience the pleasures of their intimate relationship. Whether communicated through words or touch, the couple enters into an edifying, nurturing, and satisfying experience under the affirming eye of God. In the secret haven, cloistered with only one another and their Creator,

> *A*bstaining from sex in singleness blesses the marriage with self-control, obedience, and humility. Clearly, however, it does not provide the information necessary for married couples to enjoy a satisfying sexual experience.

they welcome His presence with their attitude and actions. Each couple's secret haven should resound in praise for what God has created. There should be no feelings of guilt or shame or evil. The secret haven is a safe place of blessing and rest, and encouragement and delight.

God's plan is that the husband and wife come into marriage as virgins, never having experienced sexual contact prior to the marriage. But you may want to respond to that statement: "Well, Bunny, for goodness sake, do you realize how many couples would be disqualified if that was the standard?"

Yes, I do. But let me quickly add that even if they have missed the mark, we serve a forgiving, healing, and restoring God. His plan is always available. All we need to do is come back to it.

Especially for Singles

As a single person, once you grasp the concept of the secret haven, it will greatly aid you in seeking purity and choosing to sexually abstain before marriage. You won't want to do anything that will tarnish or damage the sacred refuge that has been set aside by the Lord for the utter enjoyment of you and your spouse. You'll take great care not to allow yourself to be put in compromising positions. As a godly single, you can learn to recognize the power of your natural desires, which will remind you how important it is to spend most of your time with the opposite sex in public places or around family and friends.

When you've properly lived out your single role, once you get married you will enter into the fulfillment promised by God. Your expectations will be realistic and informed. If you have had prior sexual activity before marriage, with your intended or with someone else, I'm sure you can recognize the importance of repenting. And let me assure you, you can walk in God's forgiveness, which makes it unnecessary to endlessly regret or unnecessarily reveal details of the past.

> *G*od has a good reason for wanting singles to abstain from sexual activity.

Before the wedding, an engaged couple should take the time to individually study a book on the human anatomy and what takes place in a man and woman's body during sexual relations. When Frank and I are involved in premarital counseling, we recommend that before their wedding night, the bride and groom agree to be sensitive to the other person's needs and to communicate openly as to what pleases and displeases them. When these steps are taken in preparation for the honeymoon, couples are able to genuinely look forward to the discoveries that lie ahead of them, without undue worries about disappointment and distress.

Unfortunately, many of us weren't blessed with appropriate premarital preparation. Perhaps you were not a wise single, and now that you are married your sex life is in awful shape. Is there hope? Yes, a million times, yes! Just keep reading. By the time you finish this book, I believe God will have given to you the tools to fix what is broken.

Entering In

It's fascinating to sit at the entrance to Disneyland and watch young children come through the gates with their parents, aunts and uncles, or grandparents. The children are oblivious to the price that was paid for them to enter that wonderland. There is one thing on their mind and that is having fun. Which way should they go? Enjoyment awaits them at every turn. While watching this unfold, I am most captivated in seeing the adults—usually fathers and mothers—taking pure delight in their children's excitement. Even while sharing the joyful anticipation, they also realize the responsibility of harnessing all that energy and leading the little ones in a constructive direction.

Saved sex is much the same. It is God's wonderland. It is a place filled with never-ending pleasures that were carefully constructed for unfolding disclosures. There is so much enjoyment in the secret haven that it takes a lifetime to discover it all. Left to our own devices, we would take a number of unproductive turns. But if we allow Him to, God will faithfully guide and direct us onto a meaningful course.

You can bet when the parents were driving their children to Disneyland they were asked at least a dozen times, "Are we there yet?" The response would probably have been on the order of, "No, Sweetie, be patient. It won't be that much longer." The wait seems to take a lifetime for children because they can't comprehend the distance to their destination. The approximate number of miles means nothing to them. There are just rows and rows of billboards, office buildings, and fast food eateries.

❧ *Especially for Singles* ❧

Singles, I think you know where I'm going here. If your desire is to be married, there's a good chance you've been sitting in the backseat of your life, feeling strapped in and constantly asking God, "Are we there yet?" The world's billboards entice you to take control and determine your own destiny. They seem to pass before your eyes every few minutes.

It is sad, but the one thing I hear most from Christian singles once they get married is they wish they had been a better single person. They regret not having lived the single season of their life in the confidence that God is indeed in the driver's seat and He knows exactly where He's going.

For those of you who are married, if sex is not exactly a Disneyland experience, you may find yourself asking God the same question: "Are we there yet?" You might be wondering if you were tricked and instead of being taken to a wonderland, you arrived at the wax museum. Everything looks real, but there is no life. Maybe your spouse is expressing impatience with you, or perhaps your struggle is an unspoken one. In any case, the sexual enjoyment you had hoped for eludes you, and there is a constant search going on in your heart, mind, and emotions for satisfaction.

When it comes to experiencing God's gift of sexuality, if you're single, it may be too early; but if you're married, it is never too late. The park of sexual pleasure remains open and available to you. The difference between it and the world's theme parks is that it is not a fantasy; it is something actually created and designed by God for us to enjoy. But there are rules and guidelines that need to be addressed. What are the rules? First of all, the admittance price is a godly marriage.

> *There* is so much enjoyment in the secret haven, it takes a lifetime to discover.

Especially for Singles

As a single person, you aren't allowed to mill around at the gate and try to get in without a ticket. The truth is you shouldn't be anywhere near the park until God takes you there. Hanging around outside and fantasizing about what's going on inside is not allowed. I think it's called loitering. If you do that, once you're married and enter the park, it's guaranteed you'll be disappointed because you will have constructed things that exist only in your imagination. Reality will be a disappointment because it won't comply with your design.

Singles who live together and feel that their love for one another should qualify them for a free pass into the park will be disappointed when they are turned away at the gate. Some of these couples have attempted to enter by scaling the fence. However, once inside the park, security guards of guilt continue to track them and lasting satisfaction is elusive.

If you're a married couple, you have a ticket to enter, and once you get there, you'll be treated like VIPs. God chauffeurs you to the park after you have said your vows. Symbolically, your marriage is a physical representation of His Son's love for the Church (Ephesians 5:23). As you go through the gate, the banner above your head does not read *"Disneyland."* No, it says *"The Secret Haven,"* and you'll quickly realize the only other person besides your spouse present is God. What is inside has been constructed for just the two of you. Careful consideration has been taken in creating a pleasurable experience. You will travel through the park for a lifetime and never run out of new vistas. God's presence fills, surrounds, and directs you. Devoted parent that He is, He smiles at your excitement and joy.

Hidden Treasures

One of the first games played upon entering the park is "hide and go seek." You and your husband begin to search out what pleases and satisfies each other. There is so much to learn. Even if you've had sexual experiences with other people prior to marriage, or premarital sex with each other, if you acknowledge your sin and repent, God forgives and restores you, so you still get to play the game. It is never too late to ask God to forgive us for our past sins. But we must always remember that the best way is to do it God's way from the beginning.

Even in the case of sexual abuse, molestation, incest, or rape, God still blesses the marriage bed. Only the perpetrator is guilty. If nonconsensual sex has taken place, the victim is not at fault. And it is important to remember that abuse or violence can happen to both men and women. If a boy is raped, it will probably go unrevealed. The level of guilt and shame cannot be comprehended, and it happens more often than we think. I have a good friend who knows of three men who, as boys, were molested by their mothers. Women aren't the only victims. Our archenemy, the devil, longs to destroy what God intended for good, and one of the devil's best schemes is to start early in a child's life. This is where saved sex takes on a very special meaning. The victim comes to realize that what is freely given and what is taken away unwillingly are two completely different things.

To get the most out of "hide and go seek," we must approach it with a teachable spirit. One of the damaging consequences of premarital sex is our preconceived notion of what satisfies our spouse. Since God was not pleased with our actions at that time, He did not sanctify the act. His help in discovering our mate was unavailable to us. But when we come to God and ask Him to lead us into the knowledge of what brings the greatest satisfaction to our spouse, He answers our prayer (in abundance). That is why it is

> *O*ne of the first games played upon entering the park is "hide and go seek."

important to remember that the wedding night is only the beginning of discovery. You won't be able to see the whole park, get on all the rides, or take in every sight. Be satisfied with whatever aspect of your spouse God allows you to enjoy. And remember—tomorrow is another day.

Every person God created comes in layers. When we first begin our sexual exploration with our spouse, our natural tendency is to run first to the fun house, where we can hide among the smoke and mirrors. The object is to find a flattering mirror and then hold our position. Hopefully, our spouse will be content with what they see and won't turn and discover the real person standing in front of the mirror. We don't want them to see our unflattering side—perhaps they will discover something unattractive. As a defense against rejection, we fight to keep our apprehensions, fears, doubt, or guilt from being exposed.

Saved sex in our secret haven makes us completely vulnerable. When we play the game, we go in search of those things that please our spouse. Sex, as God intended it, is enjoyed to the utmost when each spouse is completely transparent and open. That's why it takes a lifetime to play the game.

Our mate needs to feel protected so that he can reveal himself. If he thinks he will be exposed in a negative way, the real person will go into hiding. We have to assure our spouses that even when they stand in front of an unflattering mirror, our love for them will remain. We are willing to work with each reflection "until death do us part." The older we grow, the more the mirror's image will change. The skin may sag, but if the heart soars, our beauty will increase beyond our expectations.

So Much to Enjoy

What is an amusement park without the rides and exhibits? Some people can spend the whole day going from one ride to the next. There seems to be no roller coaster too high for them to tackle. Others are satisfied going in and out of places that have been designed to stimulate the mind or eye, like historical museums focusing on how the park was built or gift shops stocked with tons of memorabilia. How we play and what we enjoy differs. What if one spouse likes the daring rides and the other loves to just walk around? Is that a problem? No, but it is a challenge that will take patience and time to resolve. Surely there is something in the park they both enjoy. The goal is to start in that place and then slowly decide what other parts of the park will be added.

> *Sex*, as God intended it, is enjoyed to the utmost when each spouse is completely transparent and open. That's why it takes a lifetime to play the game.

Then there are the concession stands. One of the greatest reasons to attend an amusement park is to enjoy our favorite foods. Why do hot dogs just taste better when we are there? Funnel cakes, cotton candy, candy apples, and other delectable treats beckon us. In the same way, tasting God's intended goodness and experiencing His design for us in our secret haven is fulfilling. That becomes very important when we leave and return to a world that seeks to entice us with adultery and immorality.

Sitting on a park bench is relaxing. After going around the park a couple of times, rest is in order and oh, how sweet it is. Isn't it interesting that scientists have discovered that once a person is sexually satisfied, endorphins are released into the system? Those God-given healing hormones promote deep and abiding rest. He thinks of everything, doesn't He?

Crossing Over

Sex, as God created it, is a foretaste of an eternal experience. Conceptually, the intimacy (not the physical act) enjoyed between a husband and a wife will be magnified millions of times in heaven. Is it any wonder why Satan works so diligently to distort such a glorious experience? Not only does godly sexuality strengthen and edify the current relationship with our spouse, it also causes us to thirst for what awaits us on the other side of the river.

The Lord is described in Scripture as the bridegroom who rejoices over his bride (Isaiah 62:5). He's gone, "to prepare a place for us," because in His Father's house, "are many mansions" (John 14:2). He has prepared a banquet for us and our relationship with Christ will be personal and intimate. It will not include physical intimacy but commitment, purity, and ecstasy will abound.

How do you feel when you've tasted your favorite food? What pleasure flows over you when you've seen majestic beauty in God's creation? What sensations of delight cover you when a pleasant fragrance surrounds you? Can you remember the enjoyment that engulfed you when you touched something pleasurable? Do you recall a time when you heard a soothing melody and your whole body responded in delight? All of our five senses were given to us as a preview of what is to come. That eternal bliss cannot be comprehended or apprehended on earth, but now and then we have a glimpse of it, and it suggests a promise more wonderful than words can describe.

When we understand the purpose for sex and God's ultimate goal, we enter into a realm of delight and satisfaction like nothing we've known before. We approach our secret haven with overwhelming awe and gratitude. The privilege of serving a God who is so committed to our enjoyment and fulfillment overtakes us and stirs our appreciation. He intends that there should be no negative attitudes, no fear, and no guilt. Peace and contentment abound. Thanks to His grace and generosity, we are free to enter the matchless experience He has prepared for us in our secret haven.

3

Someone Is Following Me

~

*D*o you ever feel like life is a maze? Before you can discover the pleasures in your secret haven, you may find yourself navigating a never-ending path of twists and turns and dead-ends. High hedges make it impossible to see around the corners, and the lack of visibility calls the future into question. You may find yourself confused and disoriented, searching for elusive answers. Even more exasperating are the times you feel as if you're being followed—someone is tracking you in the maze. It is clear that you are not alone.

In the hidden sanctums of our mind, we are being tracked. If the culprits would just come out of the shadows and stop darting in and out, we could get a good look and identify them. But that would defeat the purpose. Their goal is to keep us distracted so truth cannot be apprehended. If they get their way, we find ourselves in such disarray that when truth approaches, fear causes us to duck behind a hedge so we can't be found.

Yes, it's true: someone or something *is* following us— lurking, peering, and planning our demise. We know and sense it but often feel helpless to defend ourselves against it. There are many examples I could draw from my life, but one stands out in particular. It is a testimony of how lies can be painted with a brush dipped in truth.

The year was 1971, and as I tried to find my way through my maze, I happened upon a psychic. His name was Ricardo. He came highly recommended, and one day he pierced my inner sanctum. My sister and I visited him at his Beverly Hills apartment. As we approached his front door, I stopped short of knocking.

My sister said, "Why are you just standing there?"

I responded, "If he's psychic, then he ought to know I'm here." Sure enough, the door opened and there stood a young man. His shoulder-length, auburn hair accented his muscular, tanned physique. Most amazing of all, he was wearing only a loincloth!

Ricardo invited us in and sat us on a rug in the middle of his sparsely furnished apartment. He handed me a pad and pen and instructed me to write down everything he said. He was going to read my future into the next seven years, and he wanted me to be able to check my notes as those years passed.

I was 21 years old, and I didn't know Christ, so this seemed like a dream come true. Ricardo began describing my life in detail. He knew names, dates, and places. During the course of our time together, he said, "You are fearful when you are standing in a bathroom and looking in a mirror while combing your hair."

> ...lies can be painted with a brush dipped in truth.

How did he know that? I had never told anyone, but that fear had been tracking me for as long as I could remember. Some of our fears seem so ridiculous we don't even try to articulate them. And what could another person say to help anyway? Somehow we know that certain things go beyond reason or logic.

It made no sense, but Ricardo knew my fear. Somehow he knew that when I stood in a bathroom, next to an open door, looking into a mirror and combing my hair, I could literally feel a hand reaching around the corner and grabbing me around my neck! In those moments, panic would engulf me, and I would break out in a cold sweat. I spent my entire time in the bathroom looking around the corner and down the hall assuring myself that no one was there.

The psychic went on to say, "In your last life—and you've had six before this one—you were a woman. As a matter a fact, you were a woman in all your past lives. One day, you were in a bathroom combing your hair, and your very jealous husband reached around the corner and strangled you. That is how you died, and that is why you have that fear."

Well, there you have it! My unknown fear was from a past life. (If you believe that, then stay with me, because the devil's lies deserve to be exposed.) Not only was Ricardo able to identify my fear, he also told me all about my roommate whom he had never met. He called her by name and stated, "She has an intense fear of the ocean." That was also true. My roommate loved to go to the beach, but she rarely left the parking lot for fear of the water.

Ricardo explained that in our last lives together, we were best friends. During that time, she became so despondent that she went to the ocean, dove into the water, and committed suicide. I went in after her but couldn't save her. She had died in the ocean. That's why she feared it.

There is no point in sharing Ricardo's other insights into my life, but they were penetrating and appeared to be true. He was very convincing. I continued to see him, and each time, I left amazed at how

"*If* he's a psychic, then he ought to know I'm here." Sure enough, the door opened and there stood a young man.

specific he was concerning the details of my life. I felt I had found the person who could lead me out of my maze. Everything he said made so much sense. I could now see clearly into my past, present, and future. There was no longer any need for me to persist in looking over my shoulder and wondering if I was still being followed.

During this same time, however, I had reached a point in my life where I had left atheism and had become agnostic. I'd progressed from believing in no God to accepting there was a supreme being who had made and loved me. I called Him my Divine Father. I woke up in the morning talking to Him, chatted with Him all day, and He was the last thing on my mind before I went to bed.

I believed my Divine Father loved me and cared about every aspect of my life. At that time, however, I did not know He had a Son. I didn't know that Jesus had died for me so I could be forgiven of all my sins and live eternally with Him. It wasn't until later that I realized God was guiding and protecting me in the maze.

Now, back to Ricardo. Two years after I began my psychic readings, in 1973, I met and married Frank Wilson. He was attracted to me because of my deep love for God. He was a Christian but had not been taught how to lead others to Christ. For a year after we were married, he loved Jesus in his heart, trusted Him, and studied the Bible while I continued to cherish my Divine Father. As counselors today, we encourage both parties to know and accept Christ before marriage so that they will not be "unequally yoked." I'm sure you can understand my overwhelming gratitude to God that He kept and protected us, in spite of our ignorance.

Frank knew about Ricardo, and shortly after our marriage, he asked me not to see him again. Frank had enough Bible training to realize that psychics were not of God, although he had to admit that many of the things Ricardo had said had come true. Although I didn't understand why

Frank was so adamant about me not seeing Ricardo, I made the decision to stop.

One day a good friend called and was threatening to commit suicide. Up to that point in my life, Ricardo had been the only solution I had to offer for problems. Yes, of course there was the Divine Father, but He was all mine. I didn't share Him with anyone. So I called Ricardo and set an appointment for her.

My friend did not have a car, so I drove. Once we got there, she insisted that I go inside with her. After Ricardo finished his reading, he turned to me and said, "Now let me read you." I declined, but he was persistent. In fact, he offered to do it for free. What decision do you think I made? You're right. He handed me a piece of paper and pen, and I began to write his words. On my note it said, "Divorced in one year...one son...affair with a Scorpio record producer."

I folded the paper, stuck it in my jacket pocket with every intention of throwing it away. Well, you've probably figured out what happened next. About two months later, I was sitting at my desk at work when the phone rang. It was Frank. "What does this note mean?" he asked. "Divorced in one year...one son...affair with a Scorpio record producer?"

I thought I was going to faint! I stuttered through an excuse of why I had gone back to Ricardo and allowed the reading. Frank was not happy. It probably didn't help that his assistant record producer was a Scorpio.

A short time later, I came into the knowledge that Jesus Christ walked the face of the earth, died on the cross for my sins, and was raised from the dead. I made the decision to repent of my sins and to ask Him to be my Lord and Savior, I was given eternal life, and I was put in right relationship with His Divine Father.

What does that have to do with the story? Becoming a Christian was and is the most important thing that has ever happened to me. It is all-encompassing. When I asked Jesus into my life, I became consumed by my love and devotion for Him. So why didn't the psychic see that coming? How did that very important event escape Ricardo's otherwise accurate predictions?

Thank God I don't have a reactionary husband. When he read the note from Ricardo, he could have become suspicious or decided to throw in the towel on our marriage. Instead, he never mentioned it again. In hindsight, it is clear that Satan had fired his best shot in an effort to strike a lethal blow early in our marriage. First Peter 5:8-9 says, "Be self-controlled and alert. Your enemy the devil prowls around like a roaring lion looking for someone to devour. Resist him, standing firm in the faith."

After being a Christian for a few years, I ran across some of the papers that listed Ricardo's view of my future. Nothing past the time I received Christ came true. I didn't divorce Frank. I didn't have an affair with a Scorpio record producer. I didn't have one son, I had five daughters. Those were just some of the things that failed to prove true.

How did Ricardo know so much about me? How could he read people I knew but he had never met? One of the answers is found in the book of Exodus. When Moses went to Pharaoh the first time and announced the Lord's command to "Let my people go" (Exodus 5:1), he threw his rod down to demonstrate God's power, and you probably remember that it turned into a snake. Very impressive! But Pharaoh's magicians had sticks too, and when they threw down their sticks, they became snakes as well. The end of the story is that Moses' snake ate all the other snakes, proving that even though the devil has power, God is all-powerful.

We are not in this world with God alone. There are unseen forces all around us, demonic beings which are very real. They can't control our free will, but being invisible gives them a great advantage. They've been around for a long time, and when they discover something about us they can use to their advantage, they find a way to whisper it in our ears. They know a great deal, based on what they have witnessed since before the world was created. They also know about past events from our private lives. The future…well, that's another story. Let's just say that whatever God allows them to touch, they will touch with their malevolent intentions, unless God says otherwise.

How much demons know and can do is a mystery, but based on the Word of God, it's quite a bit. I believe some things they just piece together. For example, let's take a look at my

> *Becoming* a Christian was and is the most important thing that has ever happened to me. It is all-encompassing. When I asked Jesus into my life, I became consumed by my love and devotion for Him. So why didn't the psychic see that coming?

fear in the bathroom. This is just one of many possible scenarios. Suppose, as a child, I saw a horror movie where a woman was strangled in the bathroom; someone's hand reached around the corner and grabbed her. Maybe Satan or one of his minions saw me hiding my face behind a pillow late that night and took note of my fright. From that day on, he could have whispered a threat each time he saw me looking around the corner of the bathroom door as I combed my hair. It was a perfect setup. I've heard it said, "Satan will flood you with truth to float one lie!"

In the same sense, Ricardo's predictions all seemed so right but were clearly wrong. There are no past lives. Hebrews 9:27 says, "Just as man is destined to die once, and after that to face judgment." We have the opportunity in this life to accept or reject God's gift in His Son, Jesus Christ, who paid the price for our sins on Calvary. That decision will determine where we spend our eternal life.

Satan used Ricardo to weave a web of lies that included not only me but also those involved in my life. Don't you think the devil knows the names of your family members and friends? Of course he does. It's easy to see how he could relay that information to a receptive, "psychic" human being.

All this prompts me to ask, "What kind of deceit is the devil working on in *your* life?"

Maybe you were raised as a Christian and taught the wisdom of avoiding psychics. That won't deter Satan. He'll just find another angle. Maybe he'll whisper thoughts to you that will lead to self-righteousness and a critical spirit. It's so easy for us to clearly see everyone else's faults while ours go undetected. Or maybe Satan is constantly reminding you about a sin that God has forgiven, but for which you cannot forgive yourself. Whatever the devil's deceptions may be, they follow us through the maze and haunt us as we approach our secret haven.

Everyone is being tracked by the devil in one way or another. Ultimately, his goal is to keep us so confused that when the hands of time stop ticking, we are condemned to eternal damnation. If, however, we do receive Jesus as our Lord and Savior and are awarded eternal life, the enemy's second plan is to disorient us so we are ineffective in surrendering ourselves to the leadership of God's Spirit.

Path to Freedom

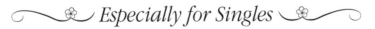

Especially for Singles

In my book *Knight in Shining Armor* I teach singles that you cannot become a successful *we* until you become a successful *me*. It's important to be complete in your single life so you can be whole in your married life. That requires you to deal with whatever is haunting your existence, whether it is seen with the natural eye or unseen in the spiritual realm.

Wouldn't it be great if two single people found their way out of the maze *before* they were joined together in holy matrimony? Wouldn't it also be terrific if they understood what to expect in their secret haven, and could spend the rest of their lives honestly discovering one another? That would be ideal, and it is exactly what God desires for us.

But what about those of us who married while we were still lost in our individual mazes? Even though we were disoriented and confused, we decided to bring a spouse in to join us. You can imagine how much havoc the devil creates in such a marriage.

Are you currently in a maze? You might be stalked by one or more of the following: confusion, anger, fear, doubt, anxiety, self-pity, despair, unforgivingness, promiscuity, pornography, masturbation, lies, deceit, or any number of other issues. Are you willing to do whatever it takes to get out? If your answer is yes, let's begin.

Thankfully, there is a path to complete freedom, a way that leads us out of the high hedges. And those who have broken through to the exit will testify that leaving the maze is exhilarating, exciting, and a great relief! In order to fully enjoy our secret haven, we must come out of the maze. Otherwise, the high hedges will overshadow what God has prepared for us.

Don't be afraid to look between the hedges of your past and uncover what is there.

Open Eyes

The first thing we have to do to get out of the maze is to open our mental and spiritual eyes and clearly see our position. Where are we? We have to identify what is going on around us and to determine the source of what is haunting us. Is it the past, the present, or the future?

When our past taunts us, we're dealing with memories, and our recollection is rarely accurate. As an adult, I recall visiting the site of the home where I was raised. Everything seemed so small; the front porch, the distance from the front door to the gate, even the "high" wall we jumped from as children seemed to have shrunk. Nothing was as big as I remembered. My memory was different than the reality because I had grown.

One of the primary troublemakers we encounter in the maze is childhood memories. Yes, there were events that shaped us as children. And some of them were just as big as they seemed. But sorting through the past requires spiritual eyes and a willingness to face the truth. Don't be afraid to look between the hedges of your past and uncover what is there. Your heavenly Father will be with you (Isaiah 41:10). Everything falls into perspective when we view things from His vantage point.

It may come as a surprise to discover that God has always been there. Even in our most difficult childhood experiences, He was with us. At first, that may anger you. "If He was there, then why did He allow me to be hurt?" you may find yourself asking. "After all, He could have prevented it!" That's where faith in a loving, sovereign God comes in. It's the place where we accept that, "all things work together for good to those who love God, to those who are called according to *His* purpose" (Romans 8:28 NKJV, emphasis added).

One of Many

There are many different issues to confront in the maze. I will select one that I believe affects everyone sometime or another in life. Do you know anyone who has not been hurt by someone else? I don't. Whether it's a family member, classmate, church member, coworker, or spouse, we have all been wounded. And the scars from our injuries still sting.

It's important to open our spiritual eyes to the need for forgiveness in every area, every situation, and with every person in our life. Unforgivingness blinds us and makes it impossible to get out of the maze. Judging another person's wrongful actions toward us causes us to walk backward as our eyes focus on the past. It forbids us to enjoy the present and distorts our future.

> *What* is haunting you? Is it the past, the present, or the future?

One of the greatest elements in forgiveness is giving up our right to judge *why* a person committed a wrongful action toward us. That does not eliminate the need to set boundaries for them, or to apply tough love when necessary. It simply means that we do unto others as God has done unto us. The Lord's Prayer becomes more than mere words when we recite, "Forgive us our trespasses *as we forgive* those who trespass against us."

Forgiveness is not optional in our attempt to get out of the maze; it is required. Once we make the decision to forgive, we begin to move forward. Before long, we face another imperative: we must attempt to be reconciled to the person who offended us. When I said "reconciliation," did I see you run and hide in the hedges? Don't stay hidden. Come out so I can explain why you need to do this to be free.

In Matthew 5 we read, "Therefore, if you are offering your gift at the altar and there remember that your brother has something against you, leave your gift there in front of the altar. First go and be reconciled to your brother; then come and offer your gift" (verses 23-24).

Is reconciliation necessary? Has someone been offended, and do they have anything against us? If so, we have to be willing to pay a call on the person, or at least telephone them, for the purpose of being reconciled. I can hear you saying, "But Bunny, I forgave them. Why do I need to go to them?"

If the person who offended you has a problem with you, Scripture requires you to try and make it right. It's important to remember that the only person you can control is yourself. The person who offended you may have unforgivingness in their heart toward you until they die. We make the attempt to reconcile because God instructs us to do so. He wants to use us as a godly example for the other person. Maybe, if we make the effort, they will also find their way out of their maze.

You may feel led to write a letter. If that's what you're thinking, think twice. You can draft a beautiful piece of correspondence and if there is one wrong word in it, the person will read it over and over again. No, you are challenged to "first *go* and be reconciled." It's important that our humility be seen or heard so that healing can begin. It is also important to note that God considers us righteous when we seek reconciliation, not when the other person forgives us. We are set free by our obedience.

*U*nforgivingness blinds us and makes it impossible to get out of the maze.

After we make the decision to reconcile, we are then able to walk toward freedom. Each step we take is made possible by unconditional love. Luke 6:35-36 reads, "Love your enemies, do good to them and lend to them without expecting to get anything back." God expects us to love and pray (Matthew 5:44, Luke 6:28) for the very people who have hurt us. By doing so, we get a taste of the great price Christ paid for us when He took upon Himself the sins of the world. Jesus loves us unconditionally.

If we are unwilling to forgive, reconcile, and walk in unconditional love, we will never get out of the maze. Have you ever taken a pencil and attempted to draw your way out of a maze on paper? Isn't it frustrating when you think you're almost at the finish line and you discover you're stuck in a dead end? Sometimes you have to go all the way back to the beginning and start again in order to find your way out. This is what will happen if you walk in unforgivingness. One of the greatest gifts you can give yourself is to forgive (give up your right to judge) someone who has hurt you.

Walking in forgiveness gives you 20/20 vision. It helps you see clearly and aids you in identifying the other areas you need to address. In the next chapter, we will continue through the maze. If you want to find your way out, keep reading. With God's help, it will happen. He is leading you toward the maze exit so you can emerge into the secret haven to enjoy all He has for you.

4

Dancing with Wolves

~

*A*s we try to find our way through life's confusing maze, we may settle comfortably into its many twists and turns. Because we're used to the surroundings, we may cease being puzzled, fearful, or conscious that someone or something is stalking us. There are times we could even forget we are there. The maze has become familiar and, since this is where we find ourselves, we might as well relax. The high hedges start feeling protective instead of like an imprisonment, and we are tempted to settle for less than the open venues of God's best for us.

Sometimes the world's beautiful music drifts through the maze and we find ourselves dancing to the tune of the piper. We go around and around in the same spot oblivious to our dance partners, who look—at first glance—like warm, safe companions. We delight in the variety of our mates as one is tapped on the shoulder by another to cut in—one imposter after another. The fact is, all too often the dance partners we meet in the maze are neither safe nor warmhearted. They are wolves dressed in sheep's clothing.

This chapter is dedicated to revealing whether or not we are dancing with wolves. God is the One who loves you most, and He will never lie to you. Because of His love, He has sought and bought you and brought you this far. Living inside of you is the Spirit of truth, waiting to unfold all the hidden mysteries of godliness and to lead you tenderly by His grace. My hope and prayer is once the wolves in your life are exposed, you will recognize them for what they are and make the decision to "dance with the One who brought you" instead.

While God could never deceive you, the ultimate imposter, who is Satan himself, will. One of his busiest and most able wolves, one who loves to get all decked out in sheep's clothing and go dancing, is called Deception. Deception's job is to make us believe something is true when it isn't. For example, Deception will lull us into thinking we have left the maze and are freely entering our secret haven, unaware that we are still lost in a lie.

First of all, Deception works very hard during our dating period to get us to downplay the sin of fornication. Then he switches his tactics and downgrades the joy of sex once you vow to become husband and wife. You seal your covenant with a kiss and God sanctions it. That is when a marriage is truly "made in heaven." Free passes to your secret haven are among one of your greatest gifts, along with having a lifelong companion and friend. Oh, that we understood marriage as God has designed it! God states, "My people are destroyed from lack of knowledge" (Hosea 4:6).

Now comes the honeymoon. Keep in mind that marriage symbolically represents Christ's love for the church. No wonder Satan hates marriage and sexual purity. Does it make Satan mad? No, it makes him furious! He spares no expense in plotting its demise, and there is no better place for deception to start than on the honeymoon. Usually the husband and wife both come with unrealistic expectations about what will take place. This accounts for the many honeymoon disasters and disappointments.

On their wedding night, most couples either travel out of town to a distant location or check into a hotel in a nearby city. And what a devil's workshop that can turn out to be! Packing and unpacking is a nuisance all by itself, not to mention the unfamiliar surroundings. Luxurious as an expensive hotel may be, all the different sights and sounds can also be quite distracting.

Hotel rooms are impersonal and the walls are not soundproof. How irritating it can be to hear people talking in the next room, to be stuck with someone else's TV blaring down the hall, or to hear the screams of little kids running up and down the halls. Add to

> "...dance with the One who brought you."

that the good possibility that you'll encounter rude service attendants at the airport or the hotel. Demons probably smile and say, "So little time and so much to do."

I'd love to hear your honeymoon story.* Some of the stories I've heard are quite funny and others quite sad. Once you have been given insight into what should have taken place, it will allow you to release any feelings of anger, bitterness, or disappointment. "I wish I had known then what I know now," may be your sentiment, but it's never too late to fix what's broken. Even if you're no longer married, your life can become richer when you see things clearly, forgive, and move on.

Especially for Singles

Singles, if you're in the process of planning a wedding, or just dreaming about one, permit me to make a suggestion. Take charge of your secret haven from day one. Perhaps following the ceremony you are scheduled to go on an exotic

---

* Write me at P.O. Box 2601, Pasadena, California 91102. Please keep details to a minimum; an overview will be just fine. However, it can do a world of good sharing what happened rather than burying it in a disappointed past.

vacation for your honeymoon or to drive to a distant location. That can wait a day or two. Meanwhile, no one needs to know that you're not leaving immediately. My advice is after the wedding, go someplace local. You can even go to the house or apartment where you will be living (if there are no out-of-town guests or family staying there).

Here's why: after the wedding, you'll be exhausted. You may be too worn-out to fully enjoy your first sexual experience, and if necessary, the two of you should agree ahead of time that falling asleep in each other's arms is perfectly okay that first night. A new morning will be awaiting you, and by the time it arrives, you'll feel rested and refreshed. But whether it's night or morning when your marriage is consummated, make sure you and your spouse are the ones in charge, and not the devil.

Should you be staying at a local hotel, take the time to check in the day before so you already have the room key. Try to get an end room away from the elevator. Then decorate the room with romantic flowers, candles, and personal pictures. Make it *your* room. Perhaps you'll want to put massage oil next to the bed and bubble bath in the bathroom. Have room service deliver some cold appetizers and beverages before you arrive. A CD player with your favorite music will add to the wonderful ambiance. And don't forget to take the telephone off the hook, and put out the "Do not disturb" sign. Also, remember not to let anyone know where you're going. Honeymoons are not the place for practical jokes from your family or friends.

> *Take charge of your secret haven from day one.*

Remember this is your *first* time of discovery. The goal should be to discover things that please your spouse. How does he want you to kiss him? How does she respond to your caresses? Go ahead, now's the time, and practice makes perfect. Before long, you can begin to discover where and how he (or she) likes to be touched in a more intimate way. I think you can figure out the rest.

If the bride is a virgin or if she has practiced abstinence for a while, the groom needs to practice restraint and be very gentle. Keep in mind that this is only the first time. Many couples are disappointed after their initial encounter because they expect full and complete satisfaction immediately. That is very difficult to accomplish because there is so much to learn. So make your minds up to relax. Have fun and take delight in your new journey of discovering the many delights embodied in your spouse.

Is It Too Late?

If you're a married woman, and you've just finished reading about the ideal honeymoon, you may be feeling a little regretful. Some questions may be troubling you: Is it too late? Hopeless? Can that fire still be ignited? Don't be deceived by the enemy's lies. The exciting answer is, "Yes! There's hope!"

The truth is, your combination lock is probably waiting to be opened. It may still be untouched. Ideally, the husband and wife should both realize where they went wrong. Wives, as I mentioned previously, chapter 10 is written just for your husband. He may not take the time to read this entire book, so I've condensed the material for him.

For now, maybe you are a married couple who never knew about the secret haven. You may have been deceived in the past, but now that you are aware, you aren't about to be denied of its pleasures! Where do you begin? Start at the beginning. If you were involved in premarital sex, then you need to repent, receive forgiveness, and let the past go. Now ask God to give you the wisdom and sensitivity to learn and discover your spouse in a new way. Take a stand against pride that suggests, "You can't teach an old dog new tricks."

You could take the time to check into a hotel and follow the plan I've suggested above for a newlywed couple. Or you may want to make some changes in your existing secret haven. Walk through the entrance to your bedroom. What do you see? Is it clean, organized, and maintained? Does it smell good? Is it decorated for both you and your husband? I once heard a masseuse say how amazed she often is when she goes into various bedrooms to do a massage. "When I look at how most bedrooms are decorated I wonder how the husband can stand it. There are so many frills and lace!"

Did you confer with your husband before you decorated the bedroom? Did he have any input with the color selection or the furniture? Maybe he said he didn't care, but what is his style? One husband told his wife he liked bold colors; red, black, and white. How do you think she decorated the bedroom? You guessed it; mauve, light green, and beige. Can the two ever agree on a design? Yes, with very careful consideration. Ladies, your husband's input on how the secret haven is decorated is important. He shouldn't feel as if he lives in *your* bedroom.

> *If* you were involved in premarital sex then you need to repent, receive forgiveness, and let the past go.

If the bedroom needs changing, it probably won't happen overnight. However, your husband will appreciate the fact that you even care. Little by little, you can start making changes.

Cleanliness is of the utmost importance and that includes your closets (stop moaning). Learn to hang up your clothes as soon as you take them off so nothing is lying around in the bedroom. Remove all work-related materials. The bedroom should be for intimate fellowship, prayer, sleep, and sex.

Soft music and lighting will create a romantic mood. Your bedroom should be your sanctuary. If you have children, they will learn from your example and carry it into their marriage. That is why it's important to get them out of your bed! How can you be intimate with your spouse when your two-year-old is sleeping between you? Your child may cry at first, but he or she will get over it and become more balanced and mature in the process.

Now let's look at your wardrobe. What do you wear in your secret haven? The long flannel nightshirt with the poodle on it has to go (unless that turns him on). Some men believe a flannel nightgown is a coded message saying, "not tonight." You should wear to bed something that pleases your spouse. A few of you may be thinking, "I'll freeze to death!" Think twice. If you really do get cold during the night, lay a warm pair of pajamas next to the bed to put on later. It's no excuse to say that you don't know what your husband prefers in lingerie. If that's a real challenge, it's time to go shopping *with* him. Find a store that will allow him to come into the dressing room, then let him choose your secret haven wardrobe.

Boy, I can feel that feminist spirit rising somewhere even as I write. Some woman has just stopped reading, and she is saying, "What? Why should I dress for *him!*"

My answer is, "Why not? You dress for other women, don't you?"

Check your closet. Who told you what colors, designs, and fabrics were in style this season? What makes you refuse to wear something because now it is "out of date"? How much time do you spend trying on clothes when you're going to have lunch with your female friends? Come on, admit it. We dress for each other. How much more should we dress to please the man we married?

Along with sight and sound, smell is important in your secret haven. If you're allergic to scents, you'll have to pass on this one. Otherwise, fragrance can be a wonderful addition. Send your husband on an excursion for his favorite women's cologne or perfume. (And once he comes home with it, be happy. It may not be your choice, but he's the one smelling it.) Let him know the only time you'll wear it is when you go to bed. Setting one scent apart from all your other perfumes and colognes will make it especially sensual.

Did you know that a large part of a woman's sexual desire is determined by her mental and emotional state? Wearing something pretty when you go to bed, spraying on a special fragrance, and preparing your bedroom for lovemaking heightens your desire. Now all you need is a husband who is on the same page.

Yesterday's News

Sometimes wives and husbands are deceived into thinking that their spouse no longer loves them. You may even believe you've both "lost that lovin' feeling." This happens when your spouse seems disinterested in finding the hidden treasure that lies waiting for him to uncover. They hardly ever look at the map any longer. What if the thrill is gone and has been for a long time? Then it's time for reflection. When did you first notice it? What was going on in your relationship at the time? Perhaps he's involved with pornography or masturbation. I'll be talking about that momentarily. Maybe he has been knocked off course by bitterness, frustration, doubt, or fear. Those are just a few of the things that can block a husband or wife's desire to visit the secret haven. We'll discuss that in the pages that follow.

Could it be that your husband thinks you disrespect him? Silence and defensiveness are definite signs that he is feeling that way.

Are you controlling and manipulative? Do you constantly contend with him? Maybe that's an example your own family set for you.

Rarely are couples able to fix what's broken overnight. But with prayer, communication, and consistency, things will change. In the thirty-first chapter of Proverbs, it says that the virtuous woman's husband trusts "she will do him good and not evil all the days of her life" (verse 12 KJV). It will take consistency on your part to get your husband to safely trust in you. But be encouraged. If he's still there, that means he's in the marriage for the long haul. With extra care and concern, I believe your marriage can grow in a new, vivacious, and victorious direction.

Not so Easy

There are other factors that can deceive us into thinking that our marriage is hopeless. Suppose one spouse is ill? What can the other spouse do? That depends on the level of their illness. What if your husband or wife is unable to perform sexually? Once again, I direct you to the book *Intended for Pleasure,* by Dr. Ed Wheat. Not only does the book give valuable information on how the body operates sexually, but the author also provides tips and techniques to aid in sexual fulfillment. If the illness is critical, then compassion must be applied.

What if you're menopausal and find that sex is uncomfortable? The first thing you need to do is see your gynecologist. A tremendous amount of research has gone into this subject, and your doctor should be able to recommend a solution for this condition.

But what if you have *no* sexual desire? Then you must go to the source. If it's a medical problem, see a doctor. If it's an emotional, spiritual, or mental problem, then see God, and discover the wonderful healing power of meditating upon and obeying His Word.

> *D*id you know that a large part of a woman's sexual desire is determined by her mental and emotional state?

When there is bitterness, anger, despair, frustration, or doubt in your life, things look different than they should. There may be times you may need the assistance of a Christian counselor. Whatever it is, get to the root and deal with it.

Perhaps your spouse has been deeply deceived by the devil, and you have discovered that he is having or has had an affair. This is such a violation of your marriage, it is difficult to overcome, but you should be aware that the Bible gives you the opportunity to leave if you so choose. However, I know many couples that have made the decision to stay together, and it is amazing how God has restored them, even after such an infraction to the relationship.

Frank and I have counseled couples who have faced up to extramarital affairs, and we have witnessed the extreme devastation such betrayal causes. If it's a consistent sexual sin, professional counseling is necessary and the guilty party has to be willing to do whatever it takes to break the addiction and regain the trust of their spouse. There is life after adultery, but it involves a conscious choice to trust in a restoring God.

To Tell the Truth

There are many ways in which a person can be deceived, but since this book is focused on sexual issues, let's deal with one that is often overlooked, excused, or denied. I'm talking about the issue of masturbation. Perhaps you haven't been tempted or been involved in this activity. If so, feel free to skip this section. But for those women or men who have participated, the following information is essential.

People who are involved in masturbation have usually convinced themselves that they are dancing alone—there's no wolf involved. They think they are hurting no one, offending no one, and accountable to no one. After all, didn't God give us the ability to satisfy our own sexual desires until we are joined in holy matrimony? No, He did not. And unfortunately, it is not *until* we are married that we realize our spouse cannot usually match our ability to satisfy ourselves.

Here's the truth this deceptive wolf won't tell you. Self-exploration and self-gratification cause us to be impatient with our husbands. Having spent much time exploring yourself may short-circuit your ability to teach your spouse the exact place, or the sensitive touch needed to bring about complete satisfaction. Because they find it difficult to match the experience of pleasing themselves, a good number of men and women continue to practice masturbation after marriage.

But that's not the only problem. Masturbation corrodes the heart, soul, and mind. Deuteronomy 6:5 says, "Love the LORD your God with *all* your heart and with *all* your soul and with *all* your strength" (emphasis added). The heart is the place where we make our decisions. The soul is the center of our emotions, and the mind is where we think our thoughts. The word "all" encompasses everything in every way.

What do people think about when they masturbate? Are their thoughts pure and holy? Could they perform the act while praying? If your answer is yes, you really are deceived. The truth is masturbation is more than a physical act—it includes a mental preparation that requires visual pictures, imaginary fantasies, and sometimes verbal expressions to stimulate the body toward climax.

Mentally, those who masturbate can be with anyone at any time: a coworker, the pastor, a friend, a neighbor, teacher, church member, even a favorite actor or musician. In their mind, they can change partners as often as they want without actually hurting anyone. No one needs to know except them.

Second Timothy 3:2 (NKJV) says, "In the last days perilous times will come: For men will be lovers themselves." Being a lover of self allows us to create what we imagine to be our own perfect partners. Imaginary lovers have no flaws. They never say anything hurtful, they are always sensitive to our needs, and they don't have bad breath! Who can compete with that vision?

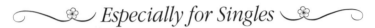

Especially for Singles

Singles, maybe you're wondering what you're supposed to do with your sexual desires. It will be necessary for you to practice one of the fruits of God's Spirit (Galatians 5:22-23)—something that will, by the way, be required of you throughout your married life. That fruit is self-control. When exercised in the single life, self-control flows over into marriage and assists us in many key areas of our marital relationship.

I cannot tell you the number of people I have counseled who have carried the pain of knowing that their spouses indulge in the self-satisfying affairs of masturbation. One woman said, "I lie next to him at night and listen while he masturbates and feel helpless to do anything about it. He refuses to discuss it with me. Instead he tells me I should try it myself!"

Especially for Singles

Single women, how can you know whether or not a prospective husband has been actively involved in masturbation prior to making the decision to marry him? First, you can never be 100 percent sure. But if you know him to be honest and trustworthy, you should be able to get the truth.

Frank and I strongly believe in premarital counseling. During this process, request that your counselor privately ask your fiancé directly about his possible involvement in masturbation and pornography. If his answer is yes, then deal with those issues before you marry him. If your prospective spouse is unwilling to address the issue, then you have a decision to make. It may be necessary for you to move on, because you can certainly expect to see other examples of his stubbornness and selfishness after you are married.

> "*In* the last days perilous times will come: For men [and women] will be lovers of themselves" (2 TIMOTHY 3:2 NKJV).

The Fantasy Fable

The maze can seem like a wonderful place when we are blinded by the lies of the dancing wolves. While you are wandering through the dark hedges, a voice whispers, "Come this way, and you will experience erotic pleasures." This appeal to our sexual hunger replaces reality, and it conceals the road sign that reads, "Dead end ahead."

The saddest part of the story is that some of those who masturbate become imprisoned by their fantasies, which haunt them day and night. One Christian sister, who is a college professor, became so addicted that she could not function on a daily basis without struggling with a pervasive need for climactic arousal.

Just how does one deal with all the thoughts that lead to erotic self-satisfaction? With God's help. But God doesn't tap on the shoulder of the wolf dressed in sheep's clothing, hoping he'll let go of you. No, He comes directly to you, taps *you* on the shoulder, and says, "Come, my daughter, let me show you the joy of purity."

If you're involved in masturbation, and the pornography that often accompanies it, you'll need to be brave enough to look behind the mask of your old dance partner. At first, the pace will probably be quickened as your partner hopes you will become dizzy and disoriented. Let me warn you, however, that you may be shocked to see what lies behind the mask—you'll find you're looking into your own face. You have been dancing with yourself!

Once you allow God to reveal the truth, you will begin to see your behavior through His eyes. Here's an example of what I mean. Suppose you are very hungry and a beautifully decorated table is wheeled in and placed in front of you. You know your favorite food is hidden under a silver dome waiting for the waiter to remove it. Putting your napkin in your lap and picking up your knife and fork, you wait in anxious anticipation. When the cover is removed, it is indeed your favorite meal. But to your horror, it is crawling with white, squirming maggots. Will you still eat it? No, I don't think so. Suddenly you no longer have an appetite.

That's how pornography and masturbation look through God's eyes. Your private fantasy is crawling with maggots of lies, selfishness, and lust. What can you do but turn away in disgust? Even though it may be one of your favorite activities, surely once you've seen it for what it is, you'll no longer want to be associated with it.

One of the biggest lies about masturbation for you, as a believer, is that even though you may have thought you were acting alone, you were never alone at all. God was always watching (2 Chronicles 16:9). Jesus was always praying (John 17:20). And the Holy Spirit, who lives inside you (John 16:13), was forced to be an unwilling participant.

For all these reasons, God is calling upon you to acknowledge that what you've been doing is a sin. According to 1 John 1:9, if you repent and confess your sin, he will forgive and cleanse you. To repent means that you acknowledge wrongdoing, turn, and go another way. As the psalmist described it, "I have considered my ways and have turned my steps to your statutes" (Psalm 119:59).

> *When* you see pornography and masturbation through God's eyes, you will turn away in disgust.

The Real World

The pleasure of sexual satisfaction is a gift God gives us, but He stores it up for us in the arms of a husband or wife. You not only need to turn *away* from pornography and/or masturbation, you also need to turn *toward* your spouse. No, he is not that perfect person lodged in your fantasy. Like you, he has flaws, but God will help you to love him anyway.

You can now direct your heart to your secret haven. There you will uncover wonderful experiences, difficult to imagine, because you will be with a real person, and a tri-dimensional one—body, soul, and spirit. As the marvelous discoveries begin, the dynamics will continue to change. Every encounter in your *secret haven* is somewhat different than the one before, because as human beings we are continually developing, growing, and expanding our awareness. Can't you see how that adds to the excitement?

Are you in a difficult marriage? I know that every marriage has its set of challenges, but in most cases, they can be fixed with the proper application of God's principles. Today, your spouse may be the most unappealing person to you in the world. That means you need a new perspective from which to view him. If you have been dancing with one of the deceptive wolves in the maze, your spouse's behavior may have changed for the worse because of his constant frustration due to rejection and disappointment.

Or perhaps your mate does not know the Lord and couldn't care less about your secret haven, your sexual needs and desires. You'll want to ask yourself whether he was uncaring when you married him. What signs did you see of that behavior or attitude while you were dating? Even though you may not have had sex before marriage, did you discuss it with him? What did he lead you to believe? Or did you get involved with fornication during your courtship and rob your secret haven of the pleasure of new discovery?

It's important to accept responsibility for how we conducted our dating and courting time. Many mistakes are made during that season and the consequences can last for a lifetime. But be encouraged—we serve a healing God, and He wants to help you with every aspect of your marriage.

It is God's intention for you to experience exciting and enjoyable sex in your secret haven. And if that's not the reality in your life, you'll want to seek the wisdom you need to reach God's goal. It may involve repentance and cleansing. It may involve forgiveness and patience. It is a journey that you have to be willing to make no matter how long it takes.

After all, you did commit to, "For better or worse, richer or poorer, in sickness and in health." And you're on the right track if you are determined to find your way out of the jumbled maze, while refusing to dance with the wolves of deception. Allowing God to guide you and living your life according to His principles will make it possible for you to find your way into the pleasures God intends for you and your spouse to share.

The Last Dance

The last dance is reserved for eternity when Christ comes for His bride (the church). There will be no more wolves and

Deception will not be invited to the ball. But until then, we can't allow ourselves to become comfortable in the maze. Our desire has to be one that keeps us focused and diligent in our pursuit to break into the clearing. Be determined to experience what God originally intended only for you and your beloved, and only within the blessed confines of your secret haven.

5

He Loves Me,
He Loves Me Not

~

*M*y friend Kathy doesn't remember a lot about her father. She buried her memories alive and left no place for a marker. That way she wouldn't have to think about his hollow laughter when he told her over and over again that she wouldn't amount to anything. She didn't have to remember the number of times he cruelly scolded her when he felt she didn't have the correct reply to his questions, or how he belittled her in front of her friends. Kathy felt no need to recall that her father was absent for every important occasion in her life, including her wedding. That was all in the past and the past was gone forever.

But there was something in Kathy's heart that continued to linger, like a candle refusing to be snuffed out. It was the tiny flame called doubt, and that doubt asked haunting questions, especially at night when the house was quiet and everyone was asleep. Constant inner misgivings challenged her belief that she could succeed and achieve her goals and dreams. And then there were those haunting questions that made her doubt her ability to love her husband and children. Kathy suffered, her family suffered, and her marriage suffered.

One of the greatest culprits hindering enjoyment in our secret haven is doubt. It freezes our emotions, leaving us frustrated and confused. It can start early in our lives, sometimes causing us to wonder whether or not our natural father loved us.

God intended for our earthly father, whom we can see, to be a physical example of our heavenly Father, whom we cannot see. When that example is distorted, it can negatively affect a child's relationship with God. "Does He really love me?" Children who have struggled with poor fathering are full of questions. "God is supposed to be everywhere, at all times and able to do all things. So why didn't He prevent bad things from happening to me? How could a God of love watch me endure hardship and suffering and rejection over and over again? Does He love me or doesn't He?"

Doubt breeds insecurity. Insecurity produces fear, and fear paralyzes us. We find ourselves behaving like the little girl who pulls petals from a daisy one by one, repeating again and again the childhood chant, "He loves me...he loves me not."

Little girls grow up into womanhood and these hindrances meet us in various ways within the secret haven. To break free of their grip, we need to reverse the order and get to know God first and intimately. Unlike man, He is flawless in every respect. When I am assured of His love, it enables me to properly view the relationship I have with my earthly father and the man who follows him—my husband. Once God is in His rightful place, my secret haven becomes unencumbered by doubt, and Frank and I are free to openly express our love.

It is easy to welcome the love of God with open arms, but why discount the fact that He is not only loving but sovereign? When we accept His sovereignty, it means we acknowledge that He is in control of everything and has the right to decide what is best for us. We have to willingly recognize that we don't have all the answers. In fact, more often than not, we don't even know how to ask the right questions.

In truth, we serve a very loving and compassionate God. And we need to be assured in the knowledge that He has a perfect plan for our lives even though there are times when things don't seem perfect at all.

You may be wondering at this point, *I thought this was a book about sex. When are we going to get back to* that? You will discover that having sex is the easy part. In order to have a lasting and satisfying sexual experience, mental, emotional, and spiritual preparation is necessary. Godly preparation is the strong foundation upon which we build, and it will endure the onslaught of life's storms and challenges.

Doubt causes us to suffer, and suffering causes us to doubt. Suffering ranks high on the list of challenges we face, because we have a tendency to constantly ask the same question over and over again: *"Why?"* We can be afflicted with physical, emotional, or mental suffering. It can come from a job, family, church, finances, health, personal relationship, or any number of other sources.

> *O*ne of the greatest culprits hindering enjoyment in our secret haven is doubt.

How great it would be if we could readily accept and apply James 1:2-4, which says, "Consider it pure joy, my brothers, whenever you face trials of many kinds, because you know that the testing of your faith develops perseverance. Perseverance must finish its work so that you may be mature and complete, not lacking anything." But we all know that is easier said than done.

Jamie, a 45-year-old mother and entrepreneur, adored her son, Mike. He was an answer to prayer for Jamie and her husband. Fortunately, Jamie operated her business out of her home and that allowed her to enjoy precious moments with Mike regularly. When her son entered high school, he was the star quarterback on the football team and a straight "A" student. His mother and father couldn't have been more proud.

Mike loved being the best, and it was important to him to stay on top. His parents worked hard for him, and he wanted to please them by earning a full scholarship to a four-year university. As he was preparing for finals in his junior year, a fellow student offered him a pill to help keep him awake. At first Mike refused, but his friend said he had taken the same kind of pill a million times. "It's perfectly safe," his friend assured him, "and it will help you cram more information into your mind. You'll get an "A"—it's a guarantee."

When Mike got a "C" on that particular test, he panicked. Now he would have to study harder than ever, and that meant keeping even later hours. He remembered the pill. He asked his friend for a few more, to get him through the school year.

When finals were over, Mike found himself fighting off depression. "No problem," said his friend, who provided him with another type of pill that would help him through those symptoms. Mike kept telling himself that he would only take the pills for just a little while, only long enough to get through this crisis. Meanwhile, Jamie noticed a change in Mike but never dreamed it was drug-related. To make a long story short, Mike ended up in a drug rehab center and, like clockwork, Jamie's whole world began to crumble.

During this same time, her business collapsed. A competitor was technologically more advanced than she was and could service customers in a much more expedient way. It wasn't long after that Jamie discovered her mother had terminal cancer.

Jamie became depressed and despondent. She asked herself again and again, "Why are these things happening to me?" Feeling defensive, she thought about the amount of time she had invested in her son. And then there was her church work and community involvement as well. She had been a loving and considerate daughter and a faithful wife. It didn't make sense to her that she would have to suffer this way.

Jamie became withdrawn and unaffectionate toward her husband. She didn't want him to touch her. "Really," she'd say as she pushed him away, "can't you see that I'm not in the mood?" She knew he wasn't to blame, but he received the brunt of her anger and frustration. Jamie didn't realize that she was making Job's mistake.

Job's Mistake

In the Old Testament, there is an accounting of a man named Job who would have understood Jamie's suffering all too well. He learned the hard way that God is sovereign even in our suffering. Understanding his story puts to rest any doubt about God's love. It will also keep us from making the same mistake Job did.

Before we return to the secret haven, let's take a close look at Job's life and glean some precious principles from all he learned. This chapter will be devoted to doing a Bible study, so grab your Bible and follow along. In chapters 1 and 2, we read about a man named Job. He is very, very rich and loves God deeply. He has always avoided evil at any cost. Then one day something very interesting happens:

> One day the angels came to present themselves before the LORD, and Satan also came with them. The LORD said to Satan, "Where have you come from?" Satan answered the LORD, "From roaming through the earth and going back and forth in it" (Job 1:6).

Satan is roaming the earth, going back and forth. That's a lot of work! What about our God? Second Chronicles 16:9 says, "The eyes of the LORD run to and fro throughout the whole earth" (KJV). It's wonderful to serve a God so powerful He doesn't even have to get up to see what is going on! Let's continue:

> Then the LORD said to Satan, "Have you con-
> sidered my servant Job? There is no one on
> earth like him; he is blameless and upright, a
> man who fears God and shuns evil." "Does
> Job fear God for nothing?" Satan replied.
> "Have you not put a hedge around him and
> his household and everything he has?…But
> stretch out your hand and strike everything he
> has, and he will surely curse you to your face."
> The LORD said to Satan, "Very well, then,
> everything he has is in your hands, but on the
> man himself do not lay a finger" (Job 1:8-12).

In chapter 1, verses 13-21, Satan destroys everything Job owns and takes the lives of his children. Does this prove that Satan can kill us and our loved ones? No, it proves that Satan is powerful, but he can do nothing without God's permission. So are we going to focus on the one who can bring destruction or the One who has the power to give him the permission? How did Job respond to his great loss? In verse 21 we find him saying, "The LORD gave and the LORD has taken away; may the name of the LORD be praised."

After this, Satan comes before God's presence again and challenges God to allow him to touch Job's body with afflic-tion. Permission is granted, and Job is covered from head to foot with boils. Does it sound like Job was just a pawn between God and Satan? Job was no pawn. God took advan-tage of the situation to mature Job and take him to a deeper spiritual level.

Three of Job's friends hear of his plight and travel a long way to encourage him. Job was so bad off that when they saw him at a distance they began to grieve. They came into his presence and sat for seven days and seven nights without saying a word. At the end of those seven days, Job speaks for all of chapter 3. You'll want to read his words.

It is clear that when Job finished speaking, his friends understood that Job was not taking any responsibility for what had happened to him. His statements so incensed them that they launched a verbal attack intended to instruct Job on why he was suffering. To get an idea how they felt read Job 4:7, 11:5, and 25:1-4.

According to Job's three friends, he was not innocent, upright, or righteous. It never dawned on them that he was suffering not because of what he had done wrong, but because of what he had done right! In all of their accusations, Job does not take responsibility for what has happened. As far as he could see, he was innocent. His friends could not prompt him to condemn himself, but they did provoke him to defend himself. That was Job's mistake, and it sorely displeased God. Job chapter 31 is called Job's defense. The whole chapter has him defending himself in light of his suffering. In verse 35, Job announces, "Oh, that I had someone to hear me! I sign now my defense—*let the Almighty answer me*" (emphasis added).

God waits seven chapters to respond. I hope you will take the time to read chapter 38. Just the first few Scriptures give you a hint of where God was headed when He says:

> Who is this that darkens my counsel with words without knowledge?...Where were you when I laid the earth's foundation?...Who marked off its dimensions?...or who laid its cornerstone?

Do you know the answer to any of the above questions? I didn't think so. Neither did Job. Can you see why Isaiah 55:8-9 says, "'For my thoughts are not your thoughts, neither are your ways my ways,' declares the LORD. 'As the heavens are higher than the earth, so are my ways higher than your ways and my thoughts than your thoughts.'"

For the same reason Proverbs 3:5-6 states, "Trust in the LORD with all your heart and lean not on your own understanding; in all your ways acknowledge him, and he will make your paths straight."

God questions Job for all of chapters 38 and 39. Finally Job responds to God in Job 40:3:

> Then Job answered the LORD, "I am unworthy— how can I reply to you? I put my hand over my mouth. I spoke once, but I have no answer—twice but I will say no more."

When I read Job's response, I thought it was a noble answer. But based on how God responded to his statement, it is clear that He was displeased. God states: "Brace yourself like a man; I will question you, and you shall answer me."

God was taking Job back to square one. It was as if He had never asked the first set of questions. Why? It is clear to God that Job *didn't get it.* He didn't understand that defending himself put God in a bad light. Those that heard Job's defense would question God's justice. They would be prompted to state, "This God that Job serves cannot be sovereign, and He definitely is not loving and kind." We know God felt this way by His next statements: "Would you discredit my justice? Would you condemn me to justify yourself?"

God then continues to ask Job questions that he could not answer for the rest of chapter 40 and all of chapter 41. At the beginning of chapter 42, Job replied again. See if you can detect the difference between this response and the first one:

> I know you can do all things; no plan of yours can be thwarted. [You asked,] "Who is this that obscures my counsel without knowledge?" Surely I spoke of things I did not understand. [You said] "Listen now, and I will speak; I will question you,"...My ears had heard of you but now my eyes have seen you....Therefore I...repent...

Did you see the comparison between how Job answered the first time and then the second? Look at his first answer. Who is Job talking about? Every statement is about himself.

> I [Job] am unworthy. How can I [Job] respond to you? I [Job] cover my hand with my mouth. I [Job] spoke once...twice but I [Job] shall say no more.

Job was turned completely inward, toward himself instead of upward, toward God. Whenever we are turned inward instead of upward, we have a challenge. In fact, no matter what is taking place in our lives, we only have one problem. It's not a singles' problem, a marriage problem, a career problem, children, ministry, or financial problem. What we have is a *God* problem! Why? Because if we saw things the way God sees them, *we wouldn't have a problem.* Remember Jamie? She, too, had turned her attention inward instead of upward. And as we've seen, it negatively affected her secret haven.

When we look at Job's second response, we see that by now, he "gets it." Look at how he has turned his focus:

> I know you [God] can do all things, no plan of yours [God's] can be thwarted...

Who is Job talking about? That's right…God. Now all his statements point upward to God. He acknowledges that God is all-knowing, all-seeing and all-powerful. His conclusion? God is sovereign!

As soon as Job repented, God stopped the questions. And when Job prayed for his friends (not about them or at them but *for* them), God healed and restored to Job everything he had lost. It's important to note that there is no indication in Scripture that God ever told Job why he suffered. Why? It appears that God was dealing with him—just as He deals with us—on a "need-to-know" basis.

Need to Know

We are soldiers in God's army. We have been dropped behind enemy lines (on earth) with the assignment to "occupy until Christ comes." If you've been in the military or watched a military movie, you know the soldiers operate on a "need-to-know" basis. Only the generals in command know every detail. That is why it's so important that "we walk by faith and not by sight" (2 Corinthians 5:7 NKJV).

God has told us all we need to know about any situation we happen to be facing. No matter what we're going through, we have enough information to see us through to victory. Let's take a look at just a couple of things "we need to know." Jeremiah 29:11 says:

> "For I know the plans I have for you," declares the LORD, "plans to prosper you and not to harm you, plans to give you hope and a future."

Does God ever *not* know what is going on in our lives? The answer, of course, is no. He is sovereign and is fully aware of everything that is taking place at all times. Therefore, we need to walk in that assurance and remind ourselves of what we need to know. 1 Thessalonians 5:18 says:

> Give thanks in all circumstances for this is
> God's will for you in Christ Jesus.

When we walk in the knowledge of God's sovereignty, we cease to doubt, in faith believing we serve a loving Father who has our best interest at heart. He announces in Isaiah 41:10:

> Do not fear, for I am with you; do not be dis-
> mayed, for I am your God. I will strengthen
> you and help you; I will uphold you with my
> righteous right hand.

Do some other Scriptures of assurance come to your mind? There are so many of them. If you are a new Christian, identify one of your challenges and then turn to the concordance (it's in the back) in your Bible and look up the word. Is it anxiety? Philippians 4:6 says:

> Do not be anxious about anything, but in
> everything, by prayer and petition, with
> thanksgiving, present your requests to God.
> And the peace of God...will guard your hearts
> and minds...

Is your problem bitterness, fear, or a relationship? Have you been crying out to God for an answer and it seems that all you get in response is silence? Perhaps God is not speaking because He has already spoken.

No matter what you are experiencing in your life, the Bible has something to say about it. Our challenge is accepting, believing, and applying God's Word to our everyday circumstances. We need to not only read the Scriptures but also to meditate upon them. That means thinking over and over again about

It appears that God deals with us on a "need-to-know" basis.

passages we've read. As we do that, God will illuminate His words for us, giving us clarity about our particular situation.

It's All Good

Job lives happily ever after, and so can you. He suffered a lot, but eventually received his just reward because he remained faithful. God "loves us...He loves us much." He will use every unpleasant experience in our lives for good. And He uses it for the good of others in His kingdom, too. Someone, somewhere is experiencing a difficult situation that is similar to yours. They need to hear an overcoming testimony. Will they hear it from you?

When we accept God's sovereignty, we approach our future with two words: "Yes, Lord!" There is no room for doubt when we are assured that God is in control of everything. From our earliest existence, He has carefully guided our steps. Even when we chose to get off the path, He was faithful to nudge us back onto the right road.

If you're single, God will instruct you about how He wants you to walk in fulfillment and assurance of His love. And if it's His desire for you to get married, He will bring your spouse to you. He will also show a willing wife how to love her husband in such a way that he lowers his guard and his heart, "safely trusts her...She does him good and not evil all the days of her life" (Proverbs 31:11-12 NKJV).

> Perhaps God is not speaking because He has already spoken.

Women need to believe in God's sovereignty in order to love their husbands the way they should. If we follow God's Word in obedience, we will honor, revere and love our husbands in spite of their present actions. It bears repeating that if physical abuse, drug abuse, or consistent sexual sin is the problem, you should seriously consider seeking Christian counseling. You will have to take a tough-love stance, but

God can still win the victory. I've heard testimony after testimony affirming His ability to heal and restore.

In most cases, however, our problems aren't so serious. The most common complaints I hear from women are a lack of affection, poor handling of finances, control, insensitivity, arrogance, and similar issues. We need to get out of God's way so He can have direct access to fixing these areas in our husbands. How do we do that? By focusing on God. We need to discover where He wants *us* to grow, rather than dwelling on the areas in which our husbands fall short.

If your earthly father was a huge disappointment, the greatest gift you can give yourself is to forgive him. Give up your right to judge why he did what he did, and release him to God. I've been through this myself—in my case, my challenge was with my mother, not my father. Both parents have a profound impact on how we love others, and especially God and our spouse. Forgiveness is essential.

When I enter my *secret* haven, I go there knowing I have a sovereign God who loves me dearly. I accept everything that has happened in my life because I realize it could not have happened without His permission. Yes, there are unanswered questions, but I have received everything I "need to know" in order to enjoy a full and complete life. If you ask and listen, the same will be true for you.

Don't allow doubt and suffering to rob you of the peace and pleasures to be found in your secret haven. I am enraptured by God's love, and it flows over into my husband. It is overwhelming to think about how passionately the Lord loves me. Experiencing the reality of my sovereign God's affection and caring allows me to see my husband through His eyes. Once I realized that the Lord loves my husband as deeply as He loves me, my husband began to look different to me. Our relationship and intimacy soared to another level. And that has given both Frank and me good reason to return again and again to our *secret haven*.

6

Sleeping Beauty

~

Within each of us is a beauty—asleep but longing to be awakened. That beauty is prayer. You will learn in this chapter that the act of sex between a husband and wife is holy and resounds with prayer. And before you decide that statement is sacrilegious, let's look together at how prayer should encompass everything we say and do.

First Thessalonians 5:17 (KJV) says, "Pray without ceasing." That means there should never be a time when we are not praying. Whether we are at home, on our job, at school, in the grocery store, driving, showering, or exercising—during every activity that consumes our day, we should be in an attitude of prayer. And that includes the time spent in the secret haven.

Whenever we turn our hearts toward God and acknowledge His presence, we are in an attitude of prayer. We should be continuously mindful that He is in, about, over, under, and through everything. God is ever-present and very near. James 4:8 states, "Come near to God and he will come near to you." Spoken prayer should simply be talking with

God. He is our Father, and He desires to fellowship with His children.

Based on these principles, it isn't out of line to say, just as prayer revolutionizes other aspects of our lives, it also revolutionizes our sex lives. When we delight in sex as God intended it to be, we share in a selfless and guilt-free experience. It is unhindered by the cares of this world, and we are able to share our deepest selves with our true love without fear. Sounds like a piece of heaven, doesn't it?

When we enter it prayerfully, our secret haven becomes consecrated because we are acutely aware of God's presence there. What we say and what we do matters to the Father. He delights in giving to us a foretaste of what awaits us in eternity. Although in heaven men and women "will neither marry nor be given in marriage" (Luke 20:35), there will be intense intimacy with our Father. We will experience complete surrender and rest in Him, consumed in our love for Him.

Just as Jesus used one earthly example after another to describe the kingdom of God, so does the intimacy between a husband and wife paint a picture of God's love for us. It creates in us a thirst to know what awaits us on the other side. The physical and spiritual connection with our spouse can no way be compared to the oneness we will have with our heavenly Father, but it is a foreshadowing. Our level of expectation is elevated and our focus becomes clearer. An overwhelming sense of gratitude encompasses us as we reflect on the awesomeness of our Creator.

> *You* will learn in this chapter that the act of sex between a husband and wife is holy, and resounds with prayer.

Lack of Understanding

If prayer is important to a satisfying sexual experience, then what do we pray and how do we pray it? For years I thought that was a perplexing question. Earlier in this book I shared how I was an atheist and feminist prior to becoming a Christian. I was very inquisitive and had questions about everything. It has always been important for me to search out the meaning of things.

Once I became a Christian that practice continued. For example, when I was confronted with the principle of submission in the Bible, my first response was, "Why would God mess up a good book with a scripture like that?"

My struggle with submission led me on a search to discover what the word meant and why God chose to base the role of a wife upon that principle. My book *Liberated Through Submission* is the fruit of that search. I discovered submission is a very positive, powerful, and aggressive principle intended for *every man and woman, single and married.*

Submission is not only a biblical principle, it is a universal principle. Webster's Dictionary defines submission as, "yielding to authority." So there is really never a question of *if* we are submitted, but rather *to whom and to what* are we submitted?

I not only struggled with the principle of submission but also the ideas of servanthood, suffering, and sacrificial love. My new struggle sent me on another search. It was interesting—Jesus was a *submitted servant* who *suffered* because of His *sacrificial love* for us, and I was struggling with the very principles that He embodied. As believers, we are commanded to walk in His footsteps. So it was essential that I come to terms with these things.

> *If* prayer is important to a satisfying sexual experience then what do we pray, and how do we pray it?

But the principle that baffled me the most in the Word of God was prayer. Although we are called to "pray without ceasing," I didn't really understand what the point was. And I certainly never dreamed it would have anything to do with the secret haven.

What caused my confusion concerning prayer? I guess I just didn't get it. Prayer didn't make sense to me. According to the Bible, God knows what we're going to say before we say it. He is already aware of our needs, and His answer is on the way, even before we ask.

In Psalm 139:4, David says, "Before a word is on my tongue you know it completely, O LORD."

In Matthew 6:8, Jesus states, "for your Father knows what you need before you ask him."

And in Isaiah 65:24, God proclaims, "Before they call I will answer."

That means He has already heard the prayer I am about to pray. Our heavenly Father sees past, present, and future all at the same time. So if God already knows what I'm going to say, then why bother to say it? Why should I pray in the first place?

In my search to understand prayer, I came to a startling conclusion: prayer is not for the purpose of informing God. It took me a long time to figure out that prayer is not so much for God's benefit as it is for ours. Prayer keeps us in constant communion and contact with our Father. It also reminds us of His faithfulness. How long do you think we would continue walking with God and trusting Him if we never brought our needs to Him?

God doesn't *need* us; He has *chosen* us. He could have dressed His angels in human form for the purpose of fellowshiping with them, and then allowed them to do His desired will. But fortunately He wants to share His glory with His created human children. When we turn our hearts toward God, we recognize that He is sovereign and in control of everything. Therefore, we shouldn't be worried about anything. In light of this, the question ceases to be, "Why pray?" and becomes, "Why *not* pray?" Instead of *having* to pray, we discover that we *get* the priviledge to pray.

Prayer inspires us to walk by faith, hoping against hope that God knows, cares, and will respond. Prayer also proclaims to the world that our trust is not in man but in God. Just before Jesus raised Lazarus from the dead, He said, "Father, I thank you that you have heard me. I knew that you always hear me, but I said this for the benefit of the people standing here" (John 11:41-42).

Just after 6 A.M. on September 11, 2001, my telephone rang and it was my 20-year-old daughter, Christy, who attends New York University. Just moments before, she happened to be looking out her window on the twenty-third floor of her apartment building, just a short distance away from the World Trade Center. She immediately began describing what she had just witnessed. An airplane had circled low and plowed directly into the World Trade Center. She'd watched it burst into flames. She couldn't believe her eyes!

When I was talking to Christy, we didn't yet know she had witnessed a terrorist attack, and we couldn't envision all the details that would filter in through our radios, newspapers, and televisions during the ensuing hours, days, and weeks. Within a short period of time, our daughter was evacuated from her building with just the clothes on her back. Christy called me on her cell phone as she was walking up the street. I could hear sirens and a great deal of commotion around her. Then the telephone went dead. Hours passed before we heard from Christy again.

For the ten minutes that followed, I felt panic rise within me, but then I began to pray in earnest. It was prayer that kept my heart and mind together during that time. My communion with God was sweet as I trusted in Him to care for Christy. That didn't mean I assumed nothing harmful would happen to her, for surely numerous believers experienced injury or lost loved ones during that terrible day. My peace came from the fact God was in control, and that He would decide what was best for Christy. She was in a win-win situation. Whether she continued to live on earth, or went to live eternally with God, I knew she would be safe.

Prayer gives us the confidence to face any situation with the knowledge that the spiritual realm controls the natural realm. We don't have to struggle or fight because God is in charge of everything. Once again, that is why Scripture exhorts us, "Do not be anxious about anything, but in everything, by prayer and petition, with thanksgiving, present your requests to God. And the peace of God, which transcends all understanding, will guard your hearts and your minds in Christ Jesus" (Philippians 4:6).

> *Prayer inspires us to walk by faith and in hope that God knows, cares, and will respond.*

When we take that mindset into our secret haven, we release a spirit of peace, and hope that all is well. Anxiety, frustration, and doubt cannot follow us there. We begin to see our spouse through the eyes of God and realize that His love for him and for us is unconditional.

Teach Me to Pray

In 1995, I began asking the Lord, "Teach me to pray." I petitioned Him again and again. Why? Because I was not happy with my prayer life. It was too formulated and impersonal. I wanted a consistent, intimate contact with my heavenly Father, and the harder I tried, the farther away He seemed to be. I read books and questioned people about how they prayed, but what they recommended just didn't work for me. I knew I was missing something, and it felt like I was dealing with an elusive butterfly. My thirst for an intimate life of prayer continued, unsated.

For years, I reminded the Lord that I didn't want anything else but to learn how to pray. Yet it felt as if my petition was falling on deaf ears, because I heard nothing. I knew prayer was the key that unlocks most doors, but I couldn't even find the door!

What puzzled me most was the Lord's Prayer (Matthew 6:9-13). I couldn't understand why, when Jesus chose to teach us how to pray, He offered such a short prayer. Just think about it. Jesus knew that what He said would be recorded for all time. Today, it would almost be equivalent to His answer being televised, simulcast, and transmitted to even the remotest sections of the world. His statements would be recorded and passed down to future generations on video, DVD, cassette, and CD. So with the camera lights in His eyes and microphones in front and above Him, Jesus knows the world is hanging on every word.

Will He tell us where to pray, the position we should take, or if our eyes should be open or shut? How about whether it is best to stand, kneel, or lie prostrate on our faces before Him? And how long should we pray—15 minutes, an hour, or half a day? Speak to us, Jesus!

To my surprise, Jesus approaches the eternal microphone and says, "And when you pray, pray like this":

Our Father in heaven, hallowed be your name,

your kingdom come, your will be done on earth as it is in heaven.

Give us today our daily bread.

Forgive us our debts, as we also have forgiven our debtors.

And lead us not into temptation, but deliver us from the evil one (Matthew 6:9-13).

That's it? That's all? That's prayer? I didn't get it. Why was it so short and lacking in detail? I have heard some say the Lord's Prayer is really found in the seventeenth chapter of John. Okay, but even there He prays first for Himself, then for His disciples, and the last seven verses are for us, the believers. We still get only seven verses, and the subject is all about unity!

Six years passed. One day while I was in my backyard pruning the juniper trees, God opened my understanding as I meditated on the Lord's Prayer. I discovered it is not a *formula*. It is, instead, a *guideline* that leads us into personal, intimate communion with our living God. Prayer is the foundation on which we build a solid walk in Christ.

The Lord's Prayer has seven sections, which I call *pillars*. These pillars take us from who, where, and what God is, to our future, present, and past, and then leads us into victory over spiritual darkness. Allow me to describe the pillars:

1 *Our Father*—describes *who* God is...

2 *in heaven*—describes *where* He is...

3 *hallowed be your name*—describes *what* He is...

4 *your kingdom come, your will be done on earth as it is in heaven*—describes the *future*...

5 *give us today our daily bread*—describes the *present*...

6 *forgive us our debts as we also have forgiven our debtors*—describes the *past*...

7 *And lead us not into temptation, but deliver us from the evil one*—describes our *spiritual victory*.

In every believer's prayer life, the pillars are the same, but what we construct in between them will be different. Our personal experience is what makes our prayer life unique. The different pains and sufferings we have tasted are common to man (and woman) (1 Peter 5:9), and they give us empathy, sympathy, and compassion toward those who have suffered like us. Our own pain compels us to "stand in the gap" for others who are hurting, because we understand their torment. And by God's grace, because of an obedient walk with Him, we have also tasted the victory of freedom from whatever bondage once held us.

The walls in between the pillars represent our experiences in life, and how we handled them becomes our stained-glass windows. As we sit in our personal prayer chapel, we view the world through that jewel-toned glass. Whether we've been through victory or defeat, it colors every event, situation, or circumstance. What we pray for and about will be impacted by what has taken place in our lives. Let's look more closely at the Lord's Prayer:

1 *Our Father...*

Jesus didn't say, "My Father." "Our Father" means that we begin our prayer remembering that we are a part of a royal family. It could have started with, "God," "Holy One," or a number of other significant recognitions, but Jesus starts the prayer with a personal and intimate acknowledgment. Jesus' words remind us that we are connected to the Father through Him, the Only Begotten One who came to pay the price for our sins.

2 *...in heaven...*

Heaven is where our Father resides, and it will eventually be our home as well. Jesus said, "in my Father's house

> The Lord's Prayer is not a *formula*. It is, instead, a *guideline* that leads us into personal, intimate communion with our living God.

are many mansions....I go to prepare a place for you. And if I go and prepare a place for you, I will come again and receive you to Myself; that where I am, *there* you may be also" (John 14:2-3 NKJV). So we begin our prayer directed up toward our Father who resides in heaven, our eternal home.

3 *...hallowed be your name.*

The very name of God is to be reverenced and adored. God has many names in the ancient Hebrew language, and each of them reveals something different about His character. We are to remember the gloriousness of His names.

4 *Your kingdom come, your will be done on earth as it is in heaven.*

Planet Earth will not always look like it does today. Revelation 21:1 says: "Then I saw a new heaven and a new earth, for the first heaven and the first earth had passed away, and there was no longer any sea." Until that takes place in the future, each believer is to be a walking, talking ambassador for what it's like in heaven. Our actions, conversations, and lifestyle should reflect the kingdom of heaven on earth.

5 *Give us today our daily bread.*

"Our daily bread" refers to everything we need to live for this particular day. In Matthew 4:4, Jesus testifies, "Man does not live on bread alone, but on every word that comes from the mouth of God." Yes, it is important to have physical food, but living a fulfilled life also includes positively feeding our minds, emotions, and spirits. On a daily basis, we need God to give us what we need to confront every situation and circumstance that faces us.

The food we eat every day is for that day alone. If we don't get consistent nourishment, our body suffers. And so it is with the mind, emotions, and soul. We need to be as committed to feeding them as we are to nurturing our physical body. That is accomplished through reading, meditating on, and applying the Word of God to our circumstances.

6 *Forgive us our debts as we have also forgiven our debtors.*

This part of the Lord's Prayer may be the most difficult for many believers. In my book *Betrayal's Baby,* I take the reader on a journey through my life. An allegory is drawn to illustrate how most of us have been betrayed by someone we loved, counted on, or believed in. And when we were betrayed, betrayal had a baby. That baby's name was Bitterness.

Time and time again, I hear Christians recount some of the events in their lives that have devastated them. Anger, bitterness, and fear abound, and they are held hostage by their emotions. In many cases, the wounds and pain are as fresh as if the damage had been done to them on that very day. But Jesus admonishes us to give up our right to judge those who have wronged us. That is exactly what He did for us on the cross when He said, "Father forgive them, for they know not what they do."

Jesus taught, "So My heavenly Father also will do to you if each of you, from his heart, does not forgive his brother his trespasses" (Matthew 18:35 NKJV). If we really believed that, we would immediately release anyone who has ever sinned against us. It means that if we're carrying unforgiveness toward anyone, we will continue to carry the weight of our own sins even though we've asked God for forgiveness. Is God still our Father? Yes. That adoption took place when we asked Jesus into our life as Lord and Savior. But our fellowship is interrupted because of our disobedience and hardness of heart.

And lead us not into temptation, but deliver us from evil.

Jesus leads us to implore God so we will be kept safe from temptation. This portion of the Lord's Prayer acknowledges and confirms the truth that we are not alone. It helps us recognize the reality of another spiritual force. Satan, formerly known as Lucifer, was the most powerful angel in heaven. He was banished to earth with one-third of God's angels when they attempted to overtake God's throne (Isaiah 14:12-15). He is pure evil, and one of his greatest advantages is that he is invisible to us. If we could see him, it would be much easier to stand firm against him.

Satan lays traps and snares. Some of them are as fine as a spider's web, and we don't even know we've been caught until we try to break free. We need our Father's assistance to keep us out of Satan's clutches.

Necessary Food

Prayer is as necessary to our mental, emotional, and spiritual life as food is to our bodies. Our souls are nourished when we acknowledge that our Father sees all, knows all, and deeply cares for each of us as His children. When we are in attitude of prayer (talking with God) throughout the day, there is a positive effect on what takes place in our secret haven. We are set free from the doubt and sorrow that chill our heart and desires. It comes as no surprise that He genuinely loves our husbands, even though—like us—they may fall short of His glory time and time again.

Prayer gives us the patience to wait while our Father fixes what is broken in our marriage. That assurance causes us to approach physical intimacy with our spouse from a positive perspective. We get to practice God's Word, up close and personal, by esteeming others better than ourselves (Philippians 2:3 NKJV).

When we step into our secret haven, we delight in the knowledge that God has prepared something special for us. Because we know that He is listening, we become conscious of the things we say aloud. Is it edifying? Does it build up? Remember, Ephesians 4:29 says, "Let no corrupt [negative and destructive] communication proceed out of your mouth, but that which is good to the use of edifying, that it may minister grace unto the hearers" (KJV).

Through prayer, active grace is applied. Grace is unmerited favor. God gives that to us in abundance every day, and He expects us to pass it on. There is no better place to do that than in our communication with our spouses. The violation of that one scriptural virtue—grace—has caused the demise of many a marriage.

> *Prayer* is as necessary to our mental, emotional, and spiritual life as food is to our bodies.

Just what has God prepared for you in your secret haven? There are sights, sounds, and sensations that can only be experienced with your spouse within the sanctity of marriage. One of these is the freedom to express and enjoy what our Father has created for His children who love Him. Each sexual encounter is a time of discovery, a time of delight, a time of release. Sometimes that may include just falling asleep in each other's arms. I love to hear my husband breathing close to my face, feeling the strength and warmth of his body near mine. I thank the Lord for every breath as I recount our day together and fall into a deep abiding rest.

Perhaps the relationship you currently have with your spouse is strained and difficult. In the next chapter that subject will be addressed. It is important now, however, for you to accept how God envisioned your time in your secret haven. I hope you are yearning for His best for you. That desire, along with applying God's Word to your marriage, can bring about wonderful results. I have watched it happen time and time again with couples we have counseled.

≈ • ≈ • ≈

Perfect Peace

Prayer leads us into God's peace, where faith and hope abide. It is so true that the "just shall walk by faith and not by sight." Romans 8:24-25 continues that thought by announcing, "Hope that is seen is no hope at all. Who hopes for what he already has? But if we hope for what we do not yet have, we wait for it patiently." It is imperative that we see our marriage through the eyes of faith and hope while abiding in an attitude of prayer. This places within us the promised peace of God, which transcends all understanding—a wonderful gift we read about in Philippians 4:7.

Remember, in chapter 1 you were challenged not to settle for anything less than saved sex. This is physical intimacy intended only for a husband and wife. Isn't it wonderful to have a personal relationship with our living God who participates in everything we say and do? As we walk in that knowledge, everything around us is illuminated with heavenly light. We are not alone in our challenges, disappointments, and frustrations. Our Father is in our midst and longs to respond to us and direct us. He does this through His Holy Spirit, who dwells in us when we accept Jesus into our hearts.

So what is my prayer life like? I begin my day on my knees, directing my thoughts and praises to the Father. When I get up, I don't walk away from His presence. At bedtime, I close my day, once again on my knees. No, my day is filled with constant recognition of His presence, and I take that with me into the secret haven.

Sleeping Beauty, in the fairy tale, is awakened when she is kissed by her beloved. The lover of her dreams envelops and holds her close to his bosom. Fears are vanquished as she listens to the beating of his heart, knowing that his love for her deepens with every breath. She is enraptured by his love and enfolded in his gentleness. Her hopes and dreams are fulfilled in his presence.

Likewise, prayer ushers us into the immediate presence of our Father. As we rest in His arms of strength and security, every care, concern, and doubt vanishes. Wrapped in His peace and snuggled in His assurance of wisdom and direction, we move through each day with quiet confidence, confronting the challenges that face us. His love flows into our secret haven, pours over us, and bathes us. There is no reason to hesitate in openly praising God for the precious gift of physical intimacy with our spouses. What an honor to be allowed to partake in God's magnificent creation. That genuine fellowship becomes an open celebration in honor of the Father's love for us.

Heavenly Father, we worship and adore Your holy and most precious name. For You are God, and beside You there is no other God. I lift up my husband to You and thank You for the gift of physical intimacy with him. May our time together in our secret haven resound in praise for You. We rejoice as we look deeply into each other's eyes and see Your love looking back at us. Thank You for the sense of touch and the ability to hear even what is unspoken. May the words of our mouth and the meditations of our hearts be acceptable in Your sight, oh Lord, our strength and our redeemer. Amen.

7

Peace Be Still

~

Why have I written this book? First, when I considered the number of years I had been robbed of experiencing physical intimacy as God intended it, I was filled with godly anger. Then as I began to touch on these struggles, it became more and more apparent I was not in the minority. There are many married couples being challenged in this area. It was also clear that a good deal of singles were also suffering in regard to the subject of sex, due to misinformation and a lack of God's vision for their lives.

Confusion and disappointment concerning sex causes unrest and disturbs our spirit. It stands contrary to God's Word, which promises us unexplainable peace. In this chapter, I want you to discover how you can experience true and lasting peace, a gentle quietness that will follow you through life no matter the circumstances.

Peace is a very necessary element in our secret haven. I have yet to meet one person who does not desire to have peace in their life. God's deep abiding peace is determined not by circumstances but in spite of them. When this peace is acquired, it fills our secret haven and allows us to totally surrender to our spouse. This same peace gives the single person sweet rest in God's love, knowing that if it is His will for them to be married, He is putting things in place to bring that to pass. If it is not His will, then they can relax in the peace of knowing He has reserved them solely for Himself during their sojourn on earth.

Peace is obtainable but it comes with a price few seem willing to pay. It requires that we take an honest look at our lives and address the strongholds and issues that face each of us. Peace demands that we identify sin in our lives such as anger, resentment, control, manipulation, sexual sins, deceit, self-pity, greed, selfishness, envy, jealousy, and many more as outlined in the Word of God. Not all the sins just mentioned apply to every person, but we know the ones that apply to us unless we are blinded to it. That is why it is necessary to ask God to reveal our open *and* hidden sins.

> *Peace* is a very necessary element in our secret haven.

An Open Mind

I remember saying to my husband some time ago, "I wish you could spend a day in my mind because then you would know how much I really love you."

Frank smiled and then voiced his concern about how he would also be able to hear any bad thoughts about him if he were to enter my mind. I assured him that even though negative thoughts did indeed hit my mind, I thought he would be pleased by how quickly they were arrested and destroyed.

It is important to not only win victory over the sin in our life but also to take control of our thought life. Peace is not possible without accomplishing both feats. One of the best books written on the battle for our mind is authored by Francis Frangipane and is entitled *The Three Battlegrounds*. I encourage you to read it.

Our secret haven is revolutionized when we take control of our thought life. So it is important to realize that our thoughts flow from two places—our mind and our heart. Our mind stores all the data recorded from the time of our birth whether heard, seen, or felt. That information governs our ability to communicate ideas. The heart records the thoughts of the mind, and it is in that place we make our heartfelt decisions.

The heart of man, according to the Bible, is not referring to the biological organ that pumps blood through our veins, but rather it is the decision-making center of our lives. Simply stated, the mind is what we think, and the heart is what we believe—both of which affect our soul, where our emotions and will live. Can you see why it is so important to put the mind and heart under God's control? When that happens, we receive the gift of "unexplainable peace." Our secret haven is dramatically impacted based on the thoughts from our mind and heart.

Romans 12:2 teaches, "Do not conform any longer to the pattern of this world, but be transformed by the renewing of your mind." God's Word teaches us a new way of thinking. Our goal should be to align our thoughts with that of our heavenly Father. We quickly discover, however, that God thinks quite differently than us for He says, "...my thoughts are not your thoughts, neither are your ways my ways....As the heavens are higher than the earth so are my ways higher than your ways and my thoughts than your thoughts" (Isaiah 55:8-9).

When we take on God's mindset, it will cause us to love those who hate us, to pray for those who spitefully use us, and to give of ourselves willingly and cheerfully. What the world defines as bondage, our Father declares as freedom. I can wholeheartedly attest to the fact that when we do things God's way, we are empowered with peace and strength.

Our mind needs to be infused with God's Word so that it can flow into our hearts. Before our heart becomes regenerated and "born again" by accepting Jesus as our Savior, the Bible teaches, "The heart is deceitful above all things and beyond cure. Who can understand it? I the LORD search the heart and examine the mind, to reward a man according to his conduct, according to what his deeds deserve" (Jeremiah 17:9).

It is almost as if we have two minds because thoughts flow from two different places. That is why James 1:8 teaches, "a double minded man is unstable in all he does" (KJV).

Have you ever been running late for a meeting and answered the telephone just before you dashed out the door? After discovering it was a friend on the other end, your mind reminded you of the importance of being polite and you complied. Somehow you found your gears switching from a fast track to a caring track as you responded, "How are you?" But even while you were asking, you had another thought that said, "I hope she doesn't tell me." Your mind said one thing, and your heart said another. The mind that stores all the data collected since we were born reminded you that it is polite to inquire about a person's well-being when you see or talk to them. I will call that the first mind. The second thought flows from the heart (the decision-making center of our life) and is controlled by either the flesh or the spirit. I will call that the second mind.

> ...the mind is what we think and the heart is what we believe—both of which affect our soul, where our emotions and will live.

Proverbs 23:7 paints another picture of the above illustration. It describes a rich ruler who has invited a man to dinner. It says, "He is the kind of man who is always thinking about the cost. 'Eat and drink,' he says to you, but his heart is not with you."

This rich man says one thing but means another, and the Bible identifies that as the sin of guile. We have to think in order to speak, but it is not the only voice we hear. During a conversation we sometimes say, "I have a second thought." We were thinking that "second thought" even while we are speaking. Understanding our two thought lives and bringing them under the lordship of Jesus Christ is what solidifies our peace.

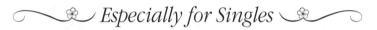

Especially for Singles

Single people, that is why it is essential that you give God time to show you what is in a potential spouse's heart. So many times we get caught up in what we hear a person saying rather than taking the time to listen to what is coming from their heart. Their second mind is what affects their ultimate behavior. First Timothy 5:22 encourages us to "lay hands suddenly on no man" (KJV).

Dedication

God's "unexplainable peace" (Philippians 4:7) is obtained through a dedicated heart. Have you ever heard of a dedicated fax machine? That fax machine has its own telephone line and does nothing but receive faxes on that number. There are also undedicated fax machines that can receive spoken and written messages on the same line.

Many hearts are like the latter example because they are constantly receiving mixed messages. But Psalm 27:8 announces, "My heart says of you [God], 'Seek his face!' Your face, LORD, I will seek." If our heart is not dedicated to receive only "good and God" thoughts, we may be swamped with messages from the flesh, and we can always count on them being self-seeking and self-serving.

A dedicated heart chooses to receive messages filtered through the Spirit and that information is undergirded by the Word of God. The flesh continues to try to break through but in 1 Peter 5:8-9 it says, "Be self-controlled and alert. Your enemy the devil prowls around like a roaring lion looking for someone to devour. Resist him, standing firm in the faith...."

As we monitor our thoughts, it's important that we arrest any negative thoughts flowing from our flesh and replace them with positive godly thoughts. Philippians 4:8-9 teaches, "Whatever is true, whatever is noble, whatever is right, whatever is pure, whatever is lovely, whatever is admirable—if anything is excellent or praiseworthy—think about such things. And the God of peace will be with you."

The years I have spent meditating on Scripture never ceases to bring me a rich reward. Notice I didn't say *memorize;* I said *meditate.* My friend, that is the key to our peace. We must hide the Word of God in our dedicated hearts so that its messages can supercede those sent from the flesh. This takes a concerted effort. If you don't know where to begin, start with some of the Scriptures quoted in this book. Or you can use a concordance to address a particular sinful thought that is plaguing you. If it is finances, look up the word money. You will find an abundance of Scriptures under that one topic.

Meditation

When you meditate on Scripture, it becomes a part of your heart. In Psalm 119:11, David says, "I have hidden your word in my heart that I might not sin against you."

A cow's eating habit is often used to illustrate the principle of meditation. A cow has four stomachs (indigestion must be a BIG problem). When it bites off a chunk of grass, the cow chews and then swallows. The grass goes down to the first stomach for a little while, and then it comes back up (I know it sounds gross but it makes the point). The cow swallows again, and it goes to the second stomach. It comes back up, and then goes to the third stomach. By the time it reaches the fourth stomach, the grass is liquid and is easily absorbed into the cow's body.

Meditating on God's Word breaks off a precious piece of truth and then chews on it until it is absorbed in the heart. Put this to the test. "The LORD is my light and my salvation— whom shall I fear?" (Psalm 27:1). This is a nice small bite of Scripture, but chew on it for a while and you will find it becoming a full-meal dish for your heart.

Meditation dissects the Scripture. Let's begin with the word "The." This word represents a particular thing. So when the Scripture says, "The Lord," it is referring to only one Lord. That reminds me of 1 Corinthians 8:6, which states, "for us there is but one God, the Father, from whom all things came and for whom we live; and there is but one Lord, Jesus Christ, through whom all

> *A*s we monitor our thoughts, it's important that we arrest any negative thoughts flowing from our flesh and replace them with positive godly thoughts.

things came and through whom we live." As we learn more and more Scriptures, they interconnect. We could stay on the word, "The" for a very long time.

Next we have the word, "The *Lord*." Boy, oh boy, do you have the time? We are talking about the Lord Jesus Christ, who is and was and is to come. The one and only "King of kings and Lord of lords." He is our Rock, Savior, Provider, and Defense. Our Lord is the King of glory! And the word that follows, "The Lord *is…*" Not *was* or *will be* but *is*. God is in the present tense—He is in the "right now" of our lives. Psalm 46:1 announces, "God *is* our refuge and strength, an ever-present help in trouble" (emphasis added). There I go connecting Scriptures again. It is so much fun! Our Lord is an "ever-present" God. He is watching you read these words right now. Can you sense His presence? Whether you can or not, He is there.

We could go on and on, but I'll stop at "The Lord is *my....*" Jesus is a personal Savior. If you had been the only one on earth, He would have still died on the cross for your sins. Scripture teaches that, "He wishes that no one be lost." I do declare that Jesus spends so much time with me I just don't know how He has time for anyone else! And yet, He spends that much time with each of His children.

> *We* must hide the Word of God in our dedicated heart so that its messages can supercede those sent from the flesh.

Meditating on the Word is fun! When I enter my kitchen to prepare dinner, I have my Bible open to the Scripture I want to meditate on. What do you think about while you're cooking? The kitchen is like a sanctuary for me. Often I'm alone and the only thing to disturb me is my thoughts. On the other hand, when I am in control of my thoughts and meditating on Scripture, there is a sweet peace that enfolds me. I meet God in my kitchen as I feast on the richness of His Word. I also meditate while I'm cleaning the house, driving my car, and exercising. It is possible to meditate on His Word "day and night," and that is what I strive to do.

We are constantly thinking about something unless we are sleeping. Have you ever paid attention to what consumes your mental space? Whatever we are thinking flows into our heart and becomes a part of what we believe. That is why we have to dedicate our heart and watch closely the thoughts we allow to enter the heart. We must be diligent to also monitor what comes in through our eyes and ears. That too becomes a part of what we think. If a woman is addicted to soap operas, she will adopt the mind-set they promote, and when she is faced with certain challenging circumstances, the information she has received from her fairy-tale TV world will flow from her mind and heart and pollute her attitudes and actions. In order to obtain peace, we must monitor what we see, hear, and think.

A Quiet Place

Our hearts and minds are treasures given to us by a great and holy God. We need to become vigilant over them while at the same time recognizing that we will be surrounded daily by challenges, irritations, and trials. I remember a day in Los Angeles when it was 105 degrees. People on the street were walking at a snail's pace. Cars without air conditioning had the windows rolled down trying to capture a breeze. Stopping at a red light, I could see the waves of heat rising from the asphalt. It was hot, but I didn't feel it. Instead I was relaxing to soft praise music and sipping on a refreshing beverage. You see, I have air conditioning in my car, and it was set at 65 degrees.

Day in and day out, we are faced with people, situations, and circumstances that can heat our emotions and frustrate our lives. We become "hot under the collar" as we rehearse scenes and statements meant to aggravate us. It can cause us to lose sleep and keep us on edge. It should come as no surprise because Jesus said, "In this world you shall have tribulation...." That portion of Scripture promises uncomfortable times, but the last part of this verse cranks up the air conditioning in our hearts: "...but be of good cheer for I have overcome the world" (John 16:33 KJV).

Is it possible to live in blessed peace in spite of what is going on around us? Yes, and yes again. I know what it means to walk in God's peace, and I have witnessed the impact that it has had on my *secret haven*. I am able to go there unrestrained and free. God's Word makes that peace available to anyone who would pursue it. That precious gift is worth every effort it takes to acquire it. Once you arrive at that place, you'll never want to leave. God does indeed, "lead us beside the still waters and restore our soul" (see Psalm 23:2-3).

In order to have peace in spite of our circumstances, we, as Christian wives, should be committed to serving our Lord by humbling ourselves to His directions concerning our marriages. Those directives are not optional, yet we are given the freedom to choose whether or not we will obey them. The choices we make, however, will determine the depth of our peace. God's ways are not our ways (Isaiah 55:8), and so it is that many things we are directed to do in His Word stand in direct opposition to the world and our flesh. In many instances it takes determined faith to obey His commands. Not to follow His guidance, however, robs us of the peace necessary to enjoy our secret haven. When we refuse to do things the Lord's way, it causes our spirit to be disturbed and creates disruption in our home.

Every now and then God gives me the privilege of mentoring a woman long distance who is having marital problems. The wife is usually stressed and despondent. I agree to mentor her on one condition: that she follow my instructions (which are rooted and based in the Word of God), and that she call only once a week to report her progress. If she has not completed her assignment for that week, she has to skip a week in contacting me. Most of these women have faced very serious challenges in their marriage. Yet there was peace in their homes within a month when they were faithful to apply God's principles. How? By taking control of their thoughts and understanding the influence God has given them with their husbands and over their homes. Never underestimate the power of the Holy Spirit in the home when unleashed through His women. Titus 2:5 states wives are "to be self-controlled and pure, to be busy at home, to be kind, and to be subject to their husbands, so that no one will malign the word of God."

First Peter 3:1 states, "Wives, in the same way be submissive to your husbands so that, *if any of them do not believe the word*, they may be *won over without words* by the behavior of their wives, when they see the purity and reverence of your lives" (emphasis added). Before you bristle at the word

> *D*ay in and day out, we are faced with people, situations, and circumstances that can heat our emotions and frustrate our lives.

"submission," take a look at the influence God has given the wife. This Scripture teaches that a husband can be won over *"without words"* by observing the behavior of his wife. How powerful is that principle? It is incredible! No muss, no fuss, just God.

If our husbands became better because of nagging, complaining, and criticizing, then who would get the credit? It most definitely would not be God. But what if a wife were consumed in loving and honoring God in her heart and actions and that caused her husband to become thirsty for God? Then who would get the credit? I have watched time and time again a husband's heart turned to God by the actions of his wife. I have also observed the wife who sees the change but, because of an undisciplined mind and heart, reverts to her old ways, leaving her husband confused. Her inconsistency also has the power to lead her husband to return to his old ways.

Warrior Wife

Peace does not come without a fight. It requires a dedicated mind and heart, a commitment to meditation, and a desire to live God's Word no matter the cost. Most of us have received many lessons on how to be the virtuous woman found in Proverbs 31, but how many of us have learned how to be the *warrior wife?* A soldier focused so intently on God's desire for our lives that we are willing to obey His commands regardless of the circumstances.

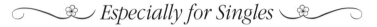

Especially for Singles

Singles, wouldn't it be wonderful if we entered marriage with the heart of a warrior wife? Whether we are married or single, we are called to be a warrior wife. Isaiah 54:5 says, "For your Maker is your husband." All the principles we have discovered in this section are valuable for our families, church members, coworkers, neighbors, and more. You need to go into marriage with a warrior-wife mentality. No, you won't be able to practice the physical intimacy part beforehand, but you will have developed the correct mindset to enjoy what God has reserved for you with your future husband. This is, of course, the ideal way for marriage to begin. Every unmarried woman has the opportunity to do it God's way and reap the rewards that He has waiting for her, while the rest of us have the privilege of starting fresh from where we are right now.

Wives, my dear sisters, and fellow laborers in God's vineyard, it is time for us to rise up and take our rightful position as warrior wives. God has given husbands the sphere of authority, but He has given wives the sphere of influence. Since God has invested in wives the sphere of influence with their husbands and home, we are given the awesome power to fill it either with peace or confusion.

Second Corinthians 10:4-6 proclaims, "The weapons we fight with are not the weapons of the world. On the contrary, they have divine power to demolish strongholds. We demolish arguments and every pretension that sets itself up against the knowledge of God, and we take captive every thought to make it obedient to Christ. And we will be ready to punish every act of disobedience, once your obedience is complete." Now that's war!

If a warrior wife were likened to a fighter plane, we would not be a B-52 or a similar plane that drops 5,000-pound bombs. No, we would be like the Stealth Bomber, which flies in under radar, bombs the enemy's position, and escapes without being detected. When our focus is off ourselves and on giving God the glory He deserves, the good that can be accomplished is immeasurable.

As a warrior wife there are many things we do that may not receive accolades because they are done in the privacy of our home and heart. No one can see when we bring a negative thought into captivity and replace it with a good one. What medals are distributed for keeping our home cleaned, organized, and maintained? Who is recording the kind and edifying words of our conversations? Perhaps in this world, recognition may come far and few between, but a warrior wife is aware that God is recording every action, thought, and word done with the right motive.

First Corinthians 3:13-14 says, "His [her] work will be shown for what it is, because the Day will bring it to light. It will be revealed with fire, and the fire will test the quality of each man's work."

A warrior wife does not live for the recognition of people, but rather, wholeheartedly serves God in all she puts her hands to. When I'm making a bed, I

> *Peace* does not come without a fight.

sometimes say to myself, "God, I'm making this bed for You." Whatever I do in word or deed, I purpose to do it for the Lord. It is a conscious decision that keeps my heart and mind focused. Do I weary sometimes? Yes. But then I remember Galatians 6:9, which says, "Let us not grow weary in well-doing, for in due season *we shall reap*, if we do not lose heart" (RSV, emphasis added).

Let's take a moment and meditate on this Scripture. "*Let us not.*" That means we shouldn't allow, tolerate, or condone the next word, which is "*grow.*" Notice that it didn't say *be* weary, it said *grow* weary. That doesn't happen overnight. It is a process that we shouldn't even allow to begin. We are instructed to grow in grace and the knowledge of our Savior. The boy Jesus grew in wisdom and favor with God and men. But to grow weary is like having a foreign substance invade your garden. How did it get there? Who planted it? Weariness is like a weed that doesn't need to be planted by anyone. It can blow in on the winds of frustration. Have you ever made a disconcerted sigh? At that moment, the seeds of weariness blew into your garden of well-doing. Or it can float down on the air of disappointment. Weariness can also be among the intentionally planted seeds of well-doing.

Frank and I once had new grass seed planted in our backyard. As it grew, it quickly became overrun with weeds. When we inquired from the gardener as to its origin, he responded that the weed seeds were mixed in the bag of grass seed. It is almost impossible to keep them out! And so it is with weariness and *well-doing.* There is always the potential for it to grow. Paul simply admonishes us to not allow it. Consequently, it is imperative that we continue to check our motives by asking ourselves why we do what we do.

Weariness, like ivy, slowly climbs around well-doing and one day chokes the life out of it. However, God has promised us that if we continue in doing good, we will reap if we don't lose heart (give up). When we apply God's principles to our lives and flesh them out, the result is sweet peace. That peace permeates our secret haven and covers our beloved with satisfaction.

8

Dreams Do Come True

~

While visiting the home of a young married woman, our conversation turned to marriage. She bubbled on about her relationship with her husband and openly began discussing their sex life. This beautiful lady shared that they had exciting sex because she always kept it fresh. For example, one day he came home and she was in the kitchen dressed as a French maid. Boy, was he surprised when he discovered what that maid had in store for him! She described different scenarios involving an array of characters she had played and proudly claimed credit for keeping the spice in their sex life. Hmmm, interesting.

Who was that sexy French maid? Why was she making love to another woman's husband? One thing was clear as she and I spoke—the woman sitting across the table from me was no French maid. She was a career woman with goals higher than parading around in frilly costumes. This unsuspecting wife was oblivious to some of the things she was putting into motion. If her husband was not prone to adultery, then she may have been helping to oust in him an appetite to sleep with other women. If the goal is to be married for a lifetime, at what point would she run out of people to play? Or how long would it take before she crossed over the line and began selecting characters like a young girl or someone else's wife?

Unfortunately, she had never been taught the beauty of saved sex. God created physical intimacy to be shared between a husband and wife so they can fully express their desire for each other and fulfill each other's dreams. A couple so enraptured by the intricacies of each other in that manner would surely take a lifetime to discover them.

Dreams Are Not Fantasies

It is okay to dream about having satisfying sexual experiences with your spouse. Notice I used the word *dream,* not *fantasize.* There is a BIG difference! The word *dream* or *dreams* is mentioned 109 times in the Bible. The word *fantasy* is never used. And even though we discussed fantasies in the earlier part of this book, we need to revisit the subject because of its far-reaching impact on our sexual intimacy.

Webster's Dictionary describes dreams as "something notable for its beauty, excellence or enjoyable quality—a strongly desired goal or purpose—something that fully satisfies a wish." Webster must have phoned heaven for God's interpretation of what it means to dream.

On the other hand, the same dictionary says a fantasy is "an imagination or fancy, especially when unrestrained." In other words, a fantasy is created images with a determined outcome, while a dream is a beautiful hope of a desire fulfilled. Someone once said, "Fantasies live in your imagination, dreams live in your heart." One is born in the dark, the other is of the light.

Especially for Singles

A godly single woman may dream of the sanctified intimacy she will one day share with her husband, but she must be careful not to fill in any details of what will take place. First of all, she cannot know for sure what will happen, and second, she is required by God to control her thought life and keep it pure.

The good news is dreams do come true, but first we must wake up and identify the dream robbers. They creep into our bed and nestle snugly in between our mate and us. Sexual satisfaction is almost impossible when they are allowed to dwell in our secret haven. These creatures fester and grow until all sexual desire is removed from either one or both of the spouses. They are invisible and insidious, but they can be destroyed. When they are identified and addressed, they will have to slink out of our secret haven and leave us to enjoy one another.

Let me introduce you to the dream robbers who might be taking up space in your bed: lies, condemnation, and guilt. All three of them take on many different forms over the years of a marriage. They consume so much space in our beds that they leave no room to move and freely enjoy our mate.

The first culprit is lies. Lies lead to confusion, and that robs us of the dream of having a satisfying sexual relationship. The definition of a lie is "an assertion of something known or believed by the speaker to be untrue with intent to deceive." This means the person making

> ...a fantasy is created images with a determined outcome, while a dream is a beautiful hope of a desire fulfilled.

the statement knows it is not true but says it anyway. Or, perhaps a lie is cooked up by the devil and served in generous portions to an unsuspecting individual who doesn't take the time to search out the truth before telling it.

For example, one lie we are told is that to keep sexual excitement in the marriage, the husband and wife should have fantasies about each other during the day so that they will be prepared to satisfy one another on a regular basis. Yet what happens when their fantasies conflict? The interesting thing about fantasizing is that the person creating the story is usually consumed with thoughts of what satisfies one's self. While the wife imagines one thing, the husband imagines another. Fantasies, by their very nature, are detailed actions that happen in a person's mind. The lie is that these fantasies will result in long-term satisfaction for the couple.

If we indulge in fantasies, we will find ourselves on a collision course with Psalm 1:2, which instructs us as to God's intention for our thought life: "His [her] delight is in the law of the LORD and on his law he meditates day and night. He is like a tree planted by streams of water, which yields its fruit in season and whose leaf does not wither. *Whatever* he does prospers" (emphasis added). And that "*whatever*" includes our sex life. We don't have time for fantasies. We should be too busy meditating on God's Word while at the same time being assured that when we enter our secret haven, enjoyment will unfold.

Back to the Garden

Dreams (hope) for sexual fulfillment are natural. God created the man and the woman to experience this delight together. Our archenemy, Satan, knows this and spends a considerable amount of time trying to direct our dreams so that we will be robbed of one of God's greatest gifts to us as a married couple. So then how do we prepare for sex with our spouse? We have to wake up.

Satan shoots fiery darts of lies into our minds (Ephesians 6:16) that many times go undetected. His goal is to make us think that we are the originator of the thought. The lie often comes in the form of a question. Satan saw it work effectively on Eve in the Garden of Eden, and it cost mankind dearly. Listen to how cleverly he played his part. "Now the serpent was more crafty than *any* of the wild animals the LORD God had made. He said to the woman, '*Did God really say*, "You must not eat from any tree in the garden"?'" (Genesis 3:1, emphasis added).

Aha! Do you see what just took place there? The devil didn't ask Eve a question, he asked her a lie. Satan knew what God had said about not eating from the forbidden tree. Instead of asking, "Did not God really say you must not eat from "*a*" tree in the garden," he said "*any*," which changes the entire meaning. The purpose of the lie was to cause confusion and to make Eve doubt God. Yet, she knew the truth because she responded, "We may eat fruit from the trees in the garden, but God did say, 'You must not eat fruit from *the* tree that is in the middle of the garden, and you must not touch it, or you will die'" (Genesis 3:2-3, emphasis added).

The devil then leads Eve to the point where he can assert his bold-faced lie to his unresistant pawn. Satan continues his game, "You will not surely die....For God knows that when you eat of it your eyes will be opened, and you will be like God, knowing good and evil." Liar, liar, pants on fire!

Eve believed the devil, ate the fruit, and then fed it to her husband. That lie cost mankind separation from God and caused confusion. Since that time, husbands and wives have been confused about many things: their roles, their responsibilities, and their God-ordained relationship. Included in that is what should take place in their secret haven.

Jesus was also confronted with one of the devil's lying questions in Luke 4:3. The devil said to him, "*If* you are the Son of God, tell this stone to become bread." Satan uses one word, "*If*" to call into question Jesus' deity. He knew Jesus was the Son of God and God the Son. Once again the goal is confusion.

If the devil used that method on Eve and Jesus, doesn't it stand to reason that he will try the same method on us? Of course he will, and I might add, it is a very successful tactic. Once lies enter our relationship, they bring with them doubt, despair, and frustration. Just like wolves, these feelings run in packs! One of our jobs as lay marriage counselors is to uncover the lies the devil has planted in each spouse's heart against the other and to reveal the truth that liberates and sets them free to love one another again.

> *The* good news is dreams do come true, but first we must wake up and identify the dream robbers.

Tim and Joyce (not their real names) are constantly at each other's throats. He believes she doesn't love him because she is unaffectionate. Joyce is convinced he doesn't love her because he is insensitive to her needs. The truth is she longs to reach out and touch him, but she *knows* that no matter how he tries to convince her otherwise, he will reject her and that freezes her ability to openly express how she feels. Meanwhile, Tim justifies not being sensitive to her needs because he prides himself on being a strong man, and reducing himself to trying to "feel what she feels" will make him a wimp. Both have believed a lie, and both are confused.

Now what about you? Has anything similar happened to you? The thought might come into your mind, *If my husband cared about me he wouldn't....* Once again notice the word *If.* When that word is inserted in our thoughts, it puts us on the path of destruction. Sometimes it takes years to unravel, but unless we get the *if* out of our marriage, it can certainly come apart. However, keep in mind that doesn't always mean it will end in divorce. Many couples stay together in a loveless union for the sake of convenience or the children. Yet just think how happy they could have been if the father of lies had not laid his head on their pillow.

Let's imagine the wife began her thought with, "*I know my husband cares about me* but *he does* (such and such)." That reflection takes her down a whole different path. Why would she choose *know* instead of *perhaps* when thinking about her husband's intentions toward her even though he may be doing something that says otherwise? Because she meditates on Romans 8:24, which says, "Hope that is seen is no hope at all. Who hopes for what he already has? But if we hope for what we do not yet have, we wait for it patiently."

She *knows* her husband cares for her because she has the *hope* that he does. In that case, she should look for things that confirm the hope. Suppose this wife continues her meditation with Philippians 4:8—"Whatever is true, whatever is noble, whatever is right, whatever is pure, whatever is lovely, whatever is admirable—if anything is excellent or praiseworthy—think about such things...And the God of peace will be with you"—what would happen?

When she focuses her attention on everything that shows he cares (even the smallest of things), this wife can then approach their challenges differently. Just because she makes the choice to think positively toward her husband does not mean that she is oblivious to an ongoing problem. She most definitely needs to address it, but in such a way that it brings life, not injury or death, to the relationship. Let me make a suggestion on how such a scenario can be handled.

Peace in the Valley

Challenges, differences, and disagreements are normal in every marriage. Two different people, two different genders, and often two different upbringings can create a tense environment for two people to live in. In order to *create* peace in the relationship, it is vital that we handle difficult or irritating situations with the utmost wisdom and care. When peace dominates a relationship, the couple look at each other in a healthy light. Even though a division exists, it is handled in such a way that their relationship is not threatened. Yes, it is ideal when both parties are practicing God's principles on how to handle division, but a tremendous impact can be felt even when just one of them is faithful in application.

Let's look at the wife who won't allow herself to think her husband does not care about her but notices a pattern of action that concerns her. Since the conclusion is he cares, she chooses to address whatever issue faces the relationship but does so in light of God's instruction.

First, she prays and asks for wisdom. "Heavenly Father, I need to see what You see and know what You know concerning this situation that is facing me with my husband. I am counting on You to lead me."

She trusts God's promise written to her,

> If any of you lacks wisdom, he [she] should ask God, who gives generously to all without finding fault, and it will be given to him. But when he asks, he must believe and not doubt, because he who doubts is like a wave of the sea, blown and tossed by the wind. That man should not think he will receive anything from the Lord; he is a double-minded man, unstable in all he does (James 1:5-6).

Here we have God's promise issued with a warning.

God will give us the wisdom to deal with whatever is facing us in our marriage. Let me repeat, Galatians 6:9 reminds us, "Let us not become weary in doing good, for at the proper time *we will reap* a harvest *if we do not give up*" (emphasis added).

Time is a crucial element as we deal with the challenges that face us in marriage. Since we are going to be married "until death do us part," we need not feel rushed in addressing the issues that concern us. Rather, we would do well to study the situation from as many angles as we can.

> *C*hallenges, differences, and disagreements are normal in every marriage.

Proverbs 15:28 says, "The heart of the righteous studies how to answer" (NKJV).

What exactly is the problem? In the past, what has her husband said to defend his position about it? The goal is to get at the root of the confusion and to hear his heart, which requires going beyond just listening to what he says. What is he not saying? Or, what has she heard him say in passing or to others that relates to the issue? What often happens is the wife is so defensive about her attitude toward it that she refuses to consider any other angle. Proverbs 21:2 says, "All a man's ways seem right to him...." Boy, was I shocked when I realized my husband might have a point when he disagreed with me on a subject.

Something I have found most interesting over the years is that many times the very thing we are condemning another person for, we are guilty of doing ourselves in other ways. Therefore, we need to take the time to say to the Lord, "God, XYZ bothers me about my husband. Am I guilty of doing something similar to him or another person?" Why should we ask that question? Because when God reveals the truth to us about our habits and actions, it gives us patience for the other person. Let me warn you that you will probably be surprised to discover how often God says, "Yes" to that prayer.

Take, for example, a husband who is hooked on golf and spends a great deal of money on the sport. His wife can't understand why he has to get a new club every time she turns around. After all, how many different ways can you hit a little white ball? Since he plays the sport often, she lives in a constant state of frustration. He appears to be addicted to the game.

But when she asks God to show her how she exhibits the same behavior, she may discover that she is just as guilty when it comes to shopping. When she drives into that mall parking lot, her eyes glaze over, and she doesn't come back to reality until she leaves. Her husband can't figure out why she needs the same pair of shoes in four different colors. When she accepts that they are both guilty of the same thing, she can adopt an attitude of humility while dealing with her husband and sympathy when she recognizes it is just as difficult for him to control his over-indulgence in golf as it is for her to control her shopping. She is no longer confused about his interest.

Another good practice I recommend before a wife addresses her husband is to spend a week acknowledging every time she is wrong. I do this within the privacy of my own heart. If I write a phone number down wrong, I admit to myself I was wrong. If I turn in the wrong direction while driving, misunderstand something that is said to me, or forget to pay the telephone bill, I admit to myself that I was wrong. Why is that a good exercise? It gets me away from thinking that I'm always right and once again adjusts my attitude when speaking to my husband about a subject on which we do not agree.

After the wife has spent a good amount of time reflecting on the challenge that faces her marriage relationship, she is ready to talk. In most cases, by the time she has studied the challenge intently, paid attention to where she falls short, and acknowledges when she is wrong, there is no anger toward her spouse and she no longer feels a sense of urgency in regard to discussing it. The perfect time for her to talk about the problem is when she doesn't feel the need to discuss it or when she doesn't want to bring it up. This means she has been able to disconnect from her passion to be right and is ready to listen.

Just because we may be guilty of a similar offense doesn't mean the issue shouldn't be addressed. When we condense what we want to say to our husbands, we will be better able to address the issues from a more congenial perspective. In other words, keep the message short.

For the most part, men are focused on the bottom line. If we really want to be heard, we need to get to the point. Setting a time to speak without distractions might sound something like this,

> *S*omething I have found most interesting over the years is that many times the very thing we are condemning another person for, we are guilty of doing ourselves in other ways.

"I know you care for me, so I thought you would want to be made aware when something negatively affects me. It will only take a few minutes. If you have something to say about the matter, I'd appreciate it if you would wait to respond until a later time so you can reflect on what I share with you. Also, if you don't mind, when I've finished, I'd like you to repeat back what I've said so that I know I've made my concern clear."

The purpose for asking for a later response is so our husbands can listen without feeling the need to defend. Then when they correctly repeat back what we said, we know they "heard" us. We proceed to share with them in reverence and respect (Ephesians 5:33) what is on our heart. I recommend that it not be longer than 3-5 minutes so that they can correctly repeat back what we've said. It's surprising how much can be communicated in that amount of time when it is thought through. After our husbands repeat back what they heard, we are then assured they have the information.

We should leave the situation alone for a while. I recommend that a month or more pass so we can continue to make observations. If we see no change, another meeting should be set, but this time with the intent of hearing his heart. We'll probably need some tissue in case what they say makes us cry, but the end result will be worth it. There is no time limit on this meeting, and at least we'll know what we are really dealing with. The key is to speak with reverence (commanded by God) and to be nondefensive.

Once again, we should start the conversation affirming our love for our husband, get to the heart of the matter, and then wait. We should listen carefully to their answer. What are we missing? I remember one day having a heart-to-heart conversation with Frank and, as I listened, I became aware that we were talking about the same issue but from two totally different perspectives. Surely he had said many of those same things over the years but I hadn't had an ear to hear. I was too consumed with only my side of the story. I didn't interrupt him nor cut him off. I considered each statement carefully and asked questions that took us deeper into the heart of the matter. The result? After a two-hour conversation, we resolved the challenge. I did cry, but not about what he shared. It happened at the very end while I was professing my deep love for him.

Frank and I put into place something that we recommend in our book, *The Master's Degree—Majoring in Your Marriage* (yes, we do follow our own advice). It is worth repeating again because it is invaluable once you have resolved an issue. It is called a "love language." A love language is a designated saying that helps us identify and pinpoint the irritant, should it repeat itself. It is a light-hearted selection of words and equips us to deal with the situation quickly the next time it occurs and many times with laughter.

For example, we were sharing this concept with a couple, and the wife pointed out something her husband did on a frequent basis that irritated her and always put her in a bad mood. The husband said it was not his intention to do so, and he didn't know when he was doing it. And so they determined from that point on, when it happened, she would say, "Honey, did you take the dog to the vet?" Now, they didn't even own a dog!

> *J*ust because we may be guilty of a similar offense doesn't mean the issue shouldn't be adressed.

This couple left the meeting with the wife equipped to handle the situation in the future and the husband not walking on eggshells hoping it didn't happen again. Sure enough, two weeks later, they attended an affair with a large number of people. This husband was talking in a circle of friends when he offended his wife. She looked at him sweetly and softly said, "Honey, did you take the dog to the vet?" Her husband looked momentarily confused, and then he remembered their agreement. He threw his head back, howled like a dog, and they both burst into laughter, much to the amazement of those standing around! He was able to pinpoint at that moment what he had done, and she was able to remind him in a lighthearted way.

After my meeting with Frank, we selected two things to say because we were dealing with two different issues, one affecting me negatively and the other him. We selected something short we would both remember, and we left that meeting on one accord, prepared to deal with the situation should it arise in the future. I must admit I was feeling very romantic towards him when the meeting was over. That is proof that a couple can talk about very serious issues without their relationship being torpedoed.

The bottom line is the devil was able to distort the truth in both our hearts, and our belief in that distortion caused us to respond and react in a way that was not pleasing to God. When we go into a time of talking about sensitive issues with our spouse and have a heart to "listen," it is amazing what we hear. It's like putting puzzle pieces together, and once the puzzle is complete, we see that the picture is the love of Christ. Confronting lies that cause confusion is absolutely mandatory when desiring to have a satisfying sex life. It clears the air and fills it with the sweet-smelling aroma of understanding.

Guilt

Another pleasure-robbing culprit is guilt. Guilt is the pilferer of freedom and the finger of condemnation. The judge, in most instances, is not God but ourselves. There are mistakes, sins, and poor judgments we have made in our lives that continue to haunt and follow us into the secret haven. Many times only ourselves and God are aware if it. Even if our spouse knows something about it, they usually will not have all the details.

For example, take a woman who is the victim of incest or molestation. Let me quickly add once again that this also happens to men. But because of pride and the fear of utter humiliation, the facts about such a past are seldom made known. These vile acts committed against a child rip at the soul. The gift of sex is torn open and smashed into little pieces. The result is usually anger, denial, low self-image, and condemnation. And the victims of incest—even though they were *victims*—often condemn themselves later on in life for allowing it to happen. They forget that they were a child and try to assess the situation from an adult perspective.

When a victim of incest, molestation, and even rape enters the secret haven, images of a painful past haunt them. There are certain things their spouse may say or do that reminds them of the violation. Just how is that hold broken? It comes when the victim accepts the truth that *saved sex* is different. They acknowledge that what was taken and what is freely given are two completely different things. They must take the steps to forgive the culprit, which means giving up their right to sit in judgment against why the violator did those awful things and releasing it all to God.* They can then allow the Lord to renew their mind and to restore them.

Another example is a woman who had an abortion and is haunted by the fact that she took an innocent life. It reminds me of Rose, who is an extraordinary woman. She has the gift of color and beauty. A banquet room filled with white tablecloths is transformed into a vision of beauty once Rose finishes decorating the room. Each table looks as if it has had a special visitation. It seems as if everything she touches becomes beautiful.

Rose is jovial and appears to be loved by everyone. The host of people who think so highly of her would be shocked to know she frequently contemplates committing suicide. It happens in the middle of the night when she often wakes up and hears a baby crying. She gets up and goes from room to room, but the baby cannot be found. Rose usually ends up in a crumpled heap agonizing over the life she took 15 years earlier. She believed the lie that it wasn't a baby in her early stages of pregnancy. Rose is suffering from post-abortion syndrome, and it manifests itself in many different ways.

The Bible teaches that life begins at conception. God says to Jeremiah in chapter 1 verse 5, "Before I formed you in the womb I knew you, before you were born I set you apart." Therefore abortion is a sin. The perpetrator is eventually consumed with guilt and post-abortion clinics acknowledge that there is a vast array of responses from the women who suffer with this guilt. Some develop suicidal tendencies or believe that anything negative happening to them is because of the sin they committed. Others fight with depression and paranoia.

---

* Forgiving an offender of incest, molestation, or rape does not negate the possibility of bringing them to justice legally. Or you may need to take a tough-love stance and expose the crime to keep others from becoming innocent victims. Seek Christian counseling and ask God to give you wisdom.

Yes, it is a sin to take a life, but it is important for the woman to know that it is a forgivable sin. There is only one sin in the Bible that is unforgivable and that is when we refuse to accept God's gift to mankind—His Son's death on the cross for our sins. Therefore, once the guilty woman confesses the sin of taking a life, she is totally forgiven, as affirmed in Psalm 103:12: "As far as the east is from the west, so far has He removed our transgressions from us."

What a gift! The east will never meet the west, which means God no longer judges her concerning the abortion.

> *Another pleasure-robbing culprit is guilt.*

Many times a woman has said to me, "But I can't forgive myself." Well, that means she is making herself greater than God. She is putting her thoughts and opinions about herself above what God's Word teaches. When she accepts God's forgiveness and rejoices in the fact that He is a God of grace (1 Peter 5:10), she walks in gratitude and freedom.

It must be quickly added, however, that with every sin comes consequences. She will have to live without ever having the pleasure of knowing the child she conceived in her womb. She may always wonder what that tiny person would have become: a scientist, a teacher, a great father or mother, and the list goes on. There may be a period of grief over the loss, but there is a big difference between grief and guilt. Grief eventually subsides, but guilt never leaves until it is extracted by Christ. And God may even use this woman to encourage expectant mothers not to abort by sharing her testimony. Truly, "we know that in all things God works for the good of those who love him, who have been called according to his purpose" (Romans 8:28).

No matter what sin we have committed, upon confession, God is, "faithful and just to forgive us our sins and cleanse us from all unrighteousness" (1 John 1:9 NKJV). To walk in that grace is a beautiful gift from our Father in heaven.

We see our secret haven in a whole other light. The glow that floods our private chambers is startlingly bright to the dream robbers as they are forced out of our bed and placed in a lineup to be identified. Lies, condemnation, and guilt attempt to hide their faces, but they have been exposed and can no longer dwell in our hearts or our place of intimacy.

In the next chapter, we will finally be prepared to meet our beloved. It will be worth the wait.

9

My Beloved

~

Come away with me, my love. My heart beats in rhythm with yours and awaits the moment when we can be together. Our secret haven has been blessed by God. When we are alone, no one but I will hear the words that come from your lips or feel the gift of your touch or see the light in your eyes. You are mine and I am yours.

There is a place where love dwells, and just walking into it can flood us with waves of joy and contentment. It soothes our senses, and delights abound. This sanctuary is free of fear, doubt, frustration, and anger. There, satisfaction awaits us and desires are fulfilled...our secret haven. This refuge is where we meet our beloved to enjoy one another in the privacy of our emotions.

Even though I have continued to include the single person in this book, in this chapter my focus will be on the married woman. For the single female, I would like to direct you to the books written by Michelle McKinney Hammond entitled *What to Do Until Love Finds You* and *Secrets of an Irresistible Woman.* For the single male I recommend *Unmasking the Lone Ranger,* authored by my husband, Frank. These books will encourage you to seek God in His

135

goodness, stretch out on His faithfulness, and reap the blessed peace that He has for those singles who seek Him.

But for now, let's spend the rest of this chapter sharing God's vision, intent, and goal for you, married ladies, as it relates to your physical relationship with your husband. My heart's desire is that you will see that sex was created by God for both your husband *and* you to pursue and enjoy.

Time Alone

Just imagine being free to walk into your secret haven without negative emotions. The sweet expectation of spending time alone with your beloved overwhelms you. The thought of once again lying in his arms and feeling his strength next to you is joy beyond measure. Truly this is a dream come true. It certainly has been my dream come true as I often have the opportunity to relish in this experience.

It has been a long road for me because I didn't have a book to walk me through the process, nor did I have a mentor to counsel me. My victory in sexual intimacy is proof positive that all we really need is God's Word and a determination to be obedient to His instructions, no matter the cost.

It has taken eight chapters of teaching to bring us to a place where we can successfully enter and enjoy the secret haven. Sustained sexual satisfaction that follows us throughout the years of our marriage does not just happen. It takes a concerted effort and determination because, as the years pass, we evolve as a couple. We will experience changes in the seasons of our lives, but even as we grow older, our secret haven never ceases to be a refuge and sanctuary.

Many are the challenges we face in marriage. There will be joy and laughter. But there will also be disappointments, discouragements, and sometimes the loss of family and friends dear to us. Careers may come and go. Eventually the children do grow up and leave the nest. There are good times and bad times, but our love for one another is meant to endure. Through it all, God's principles promise to guide us, strengthening our marriage with every adversity.

An Overview

Before we enter our secret haven to enjoy the delights that await us, I'd like to review the preparation suggestions outlined in this book. I've covered a lot of material, which I've condensed for review purposes here. This is a good time to take out a pen and check off the points that you have already implemented in your life. Of course, if there is something you have not addressed, now is the time to do so. Each item was written to have an impact on your secret haven. Let's take a look at them:

> *There* is a place where love dwells, and just walking into it can flood us with waves of joy and contentment.

- Don't settle for anything less than *saved sex!* Saved sex is more glorious than anything the world has to offer and can only be enjoyed by a man and woman joined together in holy matrimony.

- *Saved sex* is the wonderful intimacy between a Christian husband and wife, commissioned and blessed by God.

- Participating in sex as God designed it results in satisfaction for *both* partners.

- When we grasp the concept of *saved sex,* it liberates us as a married couple to completely enjoy something God created for our procreation, recreation, and communication.

- Every person's body is unique and what satisfies one may not satisfy another. *Saved sex* is devoted to exploring and discovering what pleases ourselves and our spouse.

- Even if only one person in the marriage is seeking the information concerning *saved sex,* the other spouse can be profoundly impacted.

- Sex, as God created it, is a foretaste of an eternal experience. The intimacy (not the physical act) enjoyed between a husband and wife will be magnified millions of times in heaven. Is it any wonder why Satan works so diligently to distort such a glorious experience?

It is important to grasp the concept of *saved sex.* The world cannot teach us how to satisfy our mate. It has no value system to keep sex pure. But as a born-again, blood-bought child of God, our relationship with our husband should be at a greater depth. If our desire is to love our spouse beyond his flesh and into his heart and soul, God will give us the wisdom to see into those private areas and to emotionally touch him in deep places. In order to do that, we must be free in our own emotions, and that is why the following points are so important:

- In the *secret haven,* a married couple experiences the pleasures embodied in their spouse. Whether it be spoken or expressed in touch, the couple is engaged in an edifying, nurturing, and satisfying encounter under the watchful eye of God.

- Because our archenemy, Satan, knows God's desire for the secret haven, he spends a considerable amount of time working to destroy the beauty and delights intended to be enjoyed by the married couple.

- Everyone faces some type of fear, doubt, anxiety, or rejection. Many times we must also deal with anger, guilt, and condemnation generated by past sins. In addition, unforgiveness and resentment are a hindrance in our secret haven and must be dealt with before we can fully enjoy our spouse.

- Sometimes we confuse God with our earthly parents. If our father or mother were a great disappointment to us, the greatest gift we can give ourselves is to forgive them. Unforgiveness has a profound, negative impact on our secret haven.

- Masturbation, fantasy, and/or pornography destroy the possibility of enjoying God's intent for our physical intimacy because they direct attention to satisfying one's self and thereby undermine God's structure for achieving one flesh.

> *My* victory in sexual intimacy is proof positive that all we really need is God's Word and a determination to be obedient to His instructions, no matter the cost.

- Premarital sex short-circuits the divine plan reserved for those who would keep themselves pure before marriage. Sex is the only action in the Bible that is sin before marriage and holy after marriage. It is the union under God that sanctifies the relationship. Repentance is necessary before we can experience what God had originally planned for us in our secret haven.

- Many of us welcome the love of God with open arms but discount the fact that He is sovereign. When we accept His sovereignty, it means we acknowledge He is in control of everything and has the right to decide what is best for us. Since that is true, we must hide in our heart what 1 Thessalonians 5:18 says: "Give thanks in all circumstances, for this is God's will for you in Christ Jesus." And we can cling to Romans 8:28: "We know that in all things God works to the good for those who love the Lord and are called according to His purpose."

- Sex includes prayer. First Thessalonians 5:17 says, "Pray without ceasing" (KJV). That means there should never be a time when we are not praying, even when we are in our secret haven. Whenever we turn our hearts toward God and acknowledge His presence, we are in an attitude of prayer.

- When we conclude that sex includes prayer, it revolutionizes our sex life. Our secret haven becomes holy ground as we are acutely aware of God's presence. What we say and do matters to the Father.

- God delights in our physical intimacy with our spouse, and we have the opportunity of experiencing a foretaste of what awaits us in eternity. In heaven, "people will neither marry nor be given in marriage" (Matthew 22:30), but there will be complete surrender and rest. We will also be consumed in our passionate love for God.

- It is okay to dream about having satisfying sexual experiences with your spouse. However, there is a BIG difference between dreams and fantasy. A fantasy is created images with a determined outcome, but a dream is a beautiful hope of a desire fulfilled. A dream is defined as something notable for its beauty, excellence, or enjoyable quality. This definition sums up God's desire for our sexual intimacy.

Attitude Is Everything

What we have shared concerning overcoming past guilt and condemnation along with victory over bitterness, doubt, and fear are all necessary in enjoying our secret haven. There is, however, one more necessary element that must be addressed, and that is our attitude. Since we are women of influence, our attitude speaks volumes, and this can especially be seen with our husbands.

It has been said that a man's greatest need is for respect, and I haven't met one yet that did not agree with that statement. What does vary is how they perceive respect. It is up to every wife to discover her husband's need in that area and do her best to fulfill it. Many times a wife can be in violation and not even be aware of that fact.

Do I hear a question arising? It's as if thousands of voices are chanting the same refrain and, as it draws near from off the horizon, it seems to resound in harmony. Can you hear it? A vast multitude of married women unite in one voice and ask, "WHAT ABOUT ME?"

Why, some ask, is the focus on my husband's needs and not on my own? How can I respect my husband when he does _____? I think you can fill in the blank on your own. Don't worry, our husbands aren't going to get off the hook quite so easily; the next chapter is written just for them. I know it's tempting to skip ahead at this moment and read their section, but don't do it. Stay with me so we can focus on what we should apply to our relationship *in spite* of what they do. It is imperative that we obey God's Word regardless of another person's actions.

"But, Bunny, my husband and I have issues. As a matter of fact, we have issues on our issues." Let me assure you that you will always have issues in one way or another. Obviously God did not intend for that to negatively impact our secret place.

> The wife's body does not belong to her alone but to the husband. In the same way, the husband's body does not belong to him alone but also to his wife. Do not deprave each other except by mutual consent and for a time, so that you may devote yourselves to prayer. Then come together again so Satan will not tempt you because of your lack of self control (1 Corinthians 7:4-5).

God does not list "issues" as a justification for not satisfying each other sexually. And that is understandable when we accept the fact that He has equipped us to settle our differences peacefully if we obey His instructions and guidelines for handling conflict.

One more necessary element that must be addressed is our attitude.

Issues are kind of like the environment in Los Angeles. Even if you do not live in my favorite city, you are probably well aware of our environmental issues. Living in Pasadena, a suburb, places us at the foot of the mountains. There have been days where the smog is so bad that the mountains seem to disappear.

Fortunately, the wind or the rain clears out the smog, and when that happens, Los Angeles is one of the most breathtaking cities in the world. It can remain really clear for a few days, but then slowly the smog rolls in again, and the city lights that twinkled brightly against the night's backdrop now struggle to be seen at all.

A husband and wife are two imperfect people living in an imperfect world—what a combination. The smog of our concerns may continue to roll in, but the good news is they can be cleared up. As wives, God intends for us to use our influence like a soothing rain or soft wind that clears the air.

Unfortunately, what happens far too often is our issues become like the weather. Gentle breezes can turn into thunderstorms or tornados. The lightning of our tempers strike the forest of our husband's heart and, left unchecked, thousands of acres might be destroyed before the flames are put out. Sure, new trees can be planted, but it may take years to grow back; and sometimes the forest is scorched beyond repair. The tornados of our emotions uproot trust and toss aside understanding.

Everyone has issues! The only difference is how we handle them. In the last chapter, I made a recommendation on how to deal with challenges as they arise in your marriage. Trust me, it works. I must warn you, however, that if you are waiting for all your issues to be resolved before you positively respond in your secret haven, then you may come to the end of your life and discover that you have missed the full enjoyment God intended for you.

Check the Gauge

Your secret haven takes on a special meaning when it is used as your barometer for spiritual growth. We can fool a lot of people and even ourselves into thinking we've arrived at a certain place spiritually, but the truth is revealed in our secret haven when we are alone with our husband. There is something about the physical closeness that reveals where we truly are in our hearts. When other people upset us we have the luxury of walking out, hanging up, or detaching ourselves without them being allowed to enter our space. But not so in our marriage. Our discouragement, anger, and frustration follow us to bed and sometimes the very source of them is sleeping next to us. That is when we really discover our level of spiritual maturity.

"*But*, Bunny, my husband and I have issues. As a matter of fact, we have issues on our issues."

How we handle the challenges of life comes into a bright light in our secret haven. Did you know that it is possible to have differences of opinion with your husband and face various issues without it negatively affecting your physical intimacy? That can happen when we do things God's way. Isaiah 26:3 says, "You [God] will keep in perfect peace him whose mind is steadfast because he trusts in you."

Remember the teachings in chapter 7 on the power of the mind and God's desire that we bring it under His control? Where we are mentally is revealed in our secret haven because it is hard to pretend when our husband reaches out to us for affection. Not only are we exposed mentally, but also emotionally. Any unresolved anger and frustration surfaces, and either we make it clear through our words and actions that we are not interested in being physically involved, or we suppress our emotions and pretend to be a willing participant in order to keep peace in the relationship. Both negative responses are ungodly because they would not exist if we were handling our relationship according to the Bible.

First Peter 5:6-7 states, "Humble yourselves, therefore, under God's mighty hand that he may lift you up in due time. Cast all your anxiety on him because he cares for you." The word *humble* is defined as "lacking all signs of pride, aggressiveness, or self-assertiveness." Notice that the Scripture says, "Humble *yourself*," which means God requires us to make the decision to put ourselves in that position. When we reach the point of saying, "Yes, Lord, to your way, your Word, and your will for my life," it is then that we see our issues and challenges in a different light.

Many times, however, we resist the movement of God in our lives. Rather than bowing down and allowing His mighty hand to rest upon us, we lie on our backs kicking and screaming while that same hand that is intended to cover us seems to be suffocating the life out of us.

Before we get the privilege of casting our anxiety upon the Lord, we must first humble ourselves. If we see it in picture form, we can see that as we bow down, the Lord covers us with His mighty hand and then picks us up to face Him. As He turns His hand over, there we are cradled in His palm and in a perfect position to cast all our cares upon Him.

So powerful is the rest of that portion of Scripture that I want to share it with you in its entirety. First Peter 5:6-11 proclaims:

> Humble yourselves, therefore, under God's mighty hand, that he may lift you up in due time. Cast all your anxiety on him because he cares for you. Be self-controlled and alert. Your enemy the devil prowls around like a roaring lion looking for someone to devour. Resist him, standing firm in the faith, because you know that your brothers [and sisters] throughout the world are undergoing the same kind of sufferings. And the God of all grace, who called you to his eternal glory in Christ, after you have suffered a little while, will himself restore you and make you strong, firm and steadfast. To him be the power for ever and ever. Amen.

Oh, that we would walk in God's truths! Can you see, my sister, how our secret haven reveals our level of obedience to that Scripture? God never intended for us to carry anxieties, fear, worry, and doubt in our lives or into the relationship with our husband. And when issues face us in our marriage there is a choice to be made, and our marriage becomes a barometer for how genuine that decision really is.

As I was writing this chapter, two issues surfaced between Frank and me within a week. The first one I observed for a couple of days, and then addressed it when

> *D*id you know that is is possible to have differences of opinion with your husband and face a myriad of issues without it negatively affecting your physical intimacy?

I had the proper attitude. The result was we discovered it was a misunderstanding.

The second came upon me suddenly when Frank mentioned that he wanted to inquire into a particular health insurance company with the possibility of us switching companies. The company he suggested was one I held in disdain because of reports I had heard over the years. My response was immediate and negative. We had a quick exchange of words and then abruptly halted. We looked into each other's faces and saw how our conversation was heading in a wrong direction. I apologized the next day for how I had reacted. We discussed the subject again, this time with a new attitude. The result? Well, we're still married! We're still insured! We're still lovers and friends!

In both instances, the key ingredient was *respect*. My tone, timing, and temperament set the stage for an overcoming victory or a discouraging defeat. It is worth the investment in our relationship with our husband to handle disagreements and concerns properly.

Respect for your husband follows you into your secret haven. It affects your attitude and greatly impacts his responses. Respect is given not earned. It's not an option. Ephesians 5:33 says that "the wife must respect her husband." True, Paul begins with a directive to the husband to love his wife as he loves himself; however, the two are not contingent upon each other. We each have our orders and we must obey *in spite* of our husband's decision to obey. Your husband knows when he falls short because he has the Holy Spirit to convict him. Even unsaved husbands may be "won over without words by the behavior of the wives" (1 Peter 3:1).

How can a husband who makes poor decisions be respected? Let me suggest that we respect the fact that 1 Corinthians 11:7 says, "A man...is the image and glory of God." And Philippians 1:6 states, "Being confident of this, that he who began a good work in [put your husband's name here] will carry it on to completion until the day of Christ Jesus." Respect the qualities you saw in times past, the same ones that prompted you to commit your entire life to him. They are still there even though they may have been covered up with disappointments over the years. Rehearse those qualities and attributes over and over again in your heart. Respect the decision you made to make him your husband.

Gratitude and appreciation have a significant impact on our attitude as women. "Count your blessings, name them one by one. Count your many blessings, see what God has done." This old Christian hymn reverberates an eternal truth. The next time you enter your bedroom, go with an attitude of gratitude. Do you have any idea how many single women would love to be married and enter a bedroom joined by her husband? Be grateful that you even have a bedroom. Refugees living throughout the world would be over-whelmed to have such a luxury. Appreciate that your husband is alive and that his desire is for you.

Sex can be classified as one big bundle of gratitude. Does he have the ability to touch you with his hands? Be grateful. When was the last time you hungered for his lips against yours or felt his breath intertwined with your own? Thank the Lord for every area He has placed on your body that is sensitive to your husband's touch and caress. Truly we serve an incredible God who undoubtedly had our pleasure in mind when He created man and woman.

> *R*espect for your husband follows you into your secret haven. If affects your attitude and greatly impacts his response.

It is during our time of sexual gratitude that we are able to assist by guiding and directing our husband in what pleases us. Likewise, we should be acutely aware of his desires as well. This intimate communication is meant for the two of you. What a privilege it is to know each other in that way, and to possess a secret haven that no one else can enter. It belongs only to the husband and wife joined together in holy matrimony.

Can't Get Away from It

All of what I just described involves the principles of submission, servanthood, suffering, and sacrificial love. When these four words are mentioned, what is our reaction? Whenever these words sound like fingernails on a chalkboard, we can be sure that we have fallen into the world's point of view. It is ironic that we would have a negative response, because as Christians we are called to walk in Jesus' footsteps. Our desire should be to duplicate His example while on earth. Jesus was a *submitted servant* who *suffered* because of His *sacrificial love* for us.

We have talked about submission and suffering in this book, but servanthood and sacrificial love also need to be addressed. Jesus said, "I did not come to be served but to serve." If we allowed His life to define the word *servant*, it would be a person who gives without the need for appreciation, recognition, or gratitude. Is it wrong to enjoy being noticed or appreciated? No! But a true servant serves without needing it. Everything we do is recorded in God's book, and there will be an eternal reward. When our heart's desire is to serve and please God, His applause becomes our greatest reward.

Sacrificial love demands humility. It causes us to go beyond our feelings and emotions and extends ourselves for the good of others, especially our husband. It is a powerful tool in the hand of God. "A man reaps what he sows"

(Galatians 6:7). When we esteem others better than our self (Philippians 2:4), God is magnified and His Word is glorified in us.

Rebellion, stubbornness, and contention should not be permitted to enter our secret haven. It affects our entire demeanor. Submission and respect are powerful enough to turn the hearts of the most vile men to seek the heart of God. A new man with a new heart can't help but treat his wife with the same love and respect that led him to be reconciled to God.

> All this is from God, who reconciled us to himself through Christ and gave us the ministry of reconciliation; that God was reconciling the world to himself in Christ, not counting men's sins against them. And he has committed to us the message of reconciliation. We are therefore Christ's ambassadors, as though God were making his appeal through us (2 Corinthians 5:18-20).

Remember that Ephesians 3:1 teaches that as wives we should "submit to your own husband that *even if they do not obey the word,* they may be won by observing your chaste and reverent behavior" (KJV). So great is a wife's influence over her husband that his heart can be turned to the Lord just by observing her actions and attitudes. Imagine accomplishing all that without a word!

When a husband feels respected and revered, his attitude is positively impacted, and that flows into the secret haven. "The heart of her husband safely trusts her...She does him good and not evil all the days of her life" (Proverbs 31:11 NKJV). He becomes open to revealing even the deepest part of his soul.

The next time you enter your bedroom, go with an attitude of gratitude.

It's Time

It is now time to enjoy all the delights God has placed in our secret haven. Is this the part where I give you specific instructions on what to do with your husband? No, I don't know him. And apart from you learning about his body parts, I don't believe anyone else can tell you either. This is your opportunity to explore and discover what pleases *him*.

Once we grasp God's intended vision for sex and look at our husband through His eyes, our physical desire for him falls in line. We are free to enjoy what the Lord has prepared for us. Our secret haven becomes a habitat of precious peace and enjoyment. The quest is to enjoy the wonderful delights God created for us.

Our bodies are beautiful. Sure they come in all shapes and sizes, but God was consistent in placing areas on and in our bodies that are sensitive to touch. Exploring those places takes time and communication. It is also greatly aided by the condition of your bedroom. Take a walk into your secret haven and describe what you see when you enter. Does it welcome you? Is it clean and organized? As I mentioned earlier in this book, clutter is not of God. "Let all things be done decently and in order" (1 Corinthians 14:40). His whole universe is based on order. Of course, to what degree that is maintained is relative, but there should be a semblance of order in your bedroom. Does it smell good? Is it decorated in a way that is pleasing to both you and your husband?

Perhaps your secret haven needs some work. Don't frustrate yourself. Just begin to do a little at a time. Even a "work in progress" is relaxing. Soft lighting is a bonus as well. Remember that your secret haven should minister to the senses God has placed in us.

Cleanliness is important both in the room and with our body. Bathing is not only pleasing to the smell, it is also necessary for our health. If you are able to wear a fragrance (no allergies), then allow your spouse to select the one he enjoys. I have a perfume that I wear only to bed. It has been saved and set apart for my husband alone, and I asked him to choose it.

Frank tells the story of how he was having lunch with a friend one day at a hotel. As they were paying the bill, my husband got a whiff of a wonderful

> *It* is now time to enjoy all the delights God has placed for us in our secret haven.

fragrance. He asked his friend, "Do you smell that? Where is it coming from?"

Frank's friend thought it was the lady who had just passed them, but she had gone up the stairs and was out of sight. When they settled the bill, they quickly headed in the direction they had last seen her, but she was not to be found. When they reached the valet parking, she was outside waiting for her car. Frank approached her and asked if she would mind telling him the name of the perfume she was wearing. As soon as he discovered the name, he headed for a department store with his friend in tow and purchased a bottle. I was delighted to receive it.

It's a blessing for me to know that when Frank smells a beautiful perfume on another woman the first thought he has is of me.

What a delight it is to be *known* within the confines of marriage and under God's blessing—to enjoy the presence of our spouse day after day and night after night. Does that always include having sex? No. Sometimes it encompasses a deep and meaningful conversation, while at other times it can be a soft, calm silence that rests between us. It can involve just holding hands or being in each other's presence. All of this leads up to the sweet experience that occurs in the secret haven.

When we accept that God is pleased when a married couple sexually satisfies one another, it removes any doubt and releases us to express ourselves freely. Their experience together is for them and them alone. That private closeness results in a public expression of unity and commitment. Children are able to sense the security that flows between their father and mother and witness the way they communicate and respect one another. The example is set for them to duplicate one day with their spouses.

This book was not intended to teach sexual technique. I believe that takes care of itself when the couple is absorbed with satisfying each other. If information is needed in that area, however, I once again direct you to the book authored by Dr. Ed Wheat, *Intended for Pleasure*.

My book was written to help release you and your husband emotionally, mentally, physically, and spiritually to enjoy all God created for you in the secret haven. It is also intended to equip the single person to successfully abstain from sex until marriage.

It was God, not Satan, who created sex, and He did so for procreation, communication, and recreation. And that is why there is a cross next to our bedroom door. It is there to remind us that God is there and is a part of all we say and do.

10

The Bottom Line (for Husbands Only)

~

When my husband Frank is given information, he likes to get it minus unnecessary fluff. He always wants me to get to the point, and then to give him time and space to think about what I've said. If you're a male, chances are you agree with him, so this chapter was written just for you.

First of all, allow me to sum up this book in a series of statements:

God created sex for our procreation, communication, and recreation. It is designed to be experienced by a husband and wife only. Sex is the one action in the Bible that is sinful when we are single and holy when we are married. Marriage is the joining of a man and a woman in the presence of God and witnesses in a covenant that is morally and legally binding.

God placed sensitive areas on our bodies for our pleasure, and it is your wife, not you or anybody else, who should explore and discover what satisfies you. That is why we shouldn't settle for anything less than "saved sex!" Saved sex is more glorious than anything the world has to offer, and can only be fully enjoyed by a believing husband and wife.

Satan knows the beauty and power God placed in the sexual experience and has gone to great lengths to disrupt and distort it. Every Christian husband and wife should take the responsibility of acquiring the necessary information to ensure that they are both sexually satisfied.

In this book, I refer to what I call the "secret haven." The secret haven is an area set aside where a married couple experiences the pleasures embodied in their spouse. Whether expressed in word or in touch, the couple is engaged in an edifying, nurturing, and satisfying encounter under the affirming eye of God. They are fully aware that He is present, and they welcome Him with their attitudes and actions. The secret haven should resound with our praise for what God has created. It is a sacred refuge of rest and encouragement.

What We Don't Know Can Hurt Us

Frank and I were married in 1973, and for the first five years of our marriage I pretended to be sexually satisfied. Was I trying to deceive him? No. When it came to sex, I was confused both emotionally and mentally, and I didn't think there was any help for me. I pretended to be "fine" because I loved him and didn't want him to suffer because of my inability to be satisfied. One day I confessed the truth to him, and I will be eternally grateful that his response was, "What can I do to help?" That question started us on a journey that eventually led to satisfaction for both of us.

Over the years we have counseled other couples, and Frank and I have discovered that our story is not unusual. And interestingly, it is not only wives who pretend to be

> *God* created sex for our procreation, communication, and recreation.

satisfied. When we consider how little godly information there is available on the subject of sex, is it any wonder there is so much confusion?

Who told *you* about sex? Did a loving parent with a good healthy attitude toward the subject sit down with you and paint a beautiful picture of what you would enjoy once you were married? In most cases, even if parents teach about body parts, they fall short when discussing the subject of actual sexual intimacy. Why? For the most part, it was because they didn't understand the sublime beauty in it themselves. No one has explained it to them, and they were at a loss as to what to say.

Do you have children? What have you told them about sex? If you don't explain it, just where are they supposed to find out about it? In today's society there is a wealth of information about sex, but most of it is being generated by the world and Satan. It is time for us as Christian husbands and wives to comprehend God's purpose for marital sexuality, and to be able to articulate with sensitivity the joy that awaits our children once they get married.

What the World Needs Now

The familiar lyrics of a popular song said that what the world needed was "love, sweet love." And truly, love does make the world go around. But what is love? Can it be defined? To quote my husband, "Love is seeking the highest good of the one who is the object of your affections."

For a wife, love and romance typically go hand in hand. It took Frank years to discover the secret to my heart according to *my* concept of romance. Because this is so important to pleasurable experiences in the secret haven, I have asked Frank to insert his thoughts at this point. I thought it would be beneficial for you to hear another man's perspective on this subject. So, at this time, I'd like you to meet Frank.

Frank's Thoughts About Romance

Romance is the oil that lubricates the wheels of love. This may sound poetic but trust me when I tell you it is much more than that—it is a fact. A woman, by nature, is made for romance while a man was created to be romantic. Romance is a special language that says in as many ways as possible that your wife is special to you. Words are not enough. Speech alone will fail you. If the spoken word is not accompanied by actions that communicate to her how vital, how necessary, how integral she is to your life, whatever you say will be heard as little more than hot air.

While we were in New Zealand writing *The Master's Degree*, Bunny and I had a terrible falling out about the subject of romance. I had focused on learning the breadth and scope of its dynamism, and I was writing about my ideas to other men. Yet somehow I had failed to communicate it to her—the one person who mattered most—in a way that tangibly accomplished what I was trying to say.

No matter how much you may *know* about the definition of romance, if you do not *understand* the intimate needs of your wife, your knowledge is useless. It would be like creating a ripple in the water from the shore that never touches the ship where she is reclining on the top deck, waiting to hear from you. How to reach her is the key; how to find the ability to say, "You are my other self," so that she knows her worth to you, is priceless.

Someone has wisely said that the greatest thing a father can do for his children is to allow them to see him loving their mother. This is clearly demonstrated in romantic expressions that take place all around the house. Proverbs compares romance to mysteries such as the *ways of a ship on the open seas, an eagle floating upon the currents of invisible air, and a snake, without the assistance of tentacles, moving effortlessly over smoothly polished rocks.* To gain an understanding of this, one must go to God, the One who created us all. He says, *"Husbands, dwell with them [your wives] according to knowledge"* (1 Peter 3:7 KJV, emphasis added).

After an initial period of physical attraction, the excitement of courtship, and the newness of a marriage, romance has to develop a long-range view that will keep passion alive. Like a laser beam fastened upon its target, romance zeros in, past all deterrents and common problems of flawed personalities. At last, it finds its defenseless prey caught in the thickets of unfettered admiration.

The following is how I would view your timely pursuit:

A wise husband follows the footsteps of his own beating heart, listening until his wife is captured. Then he starts the occupation all over again, daring her to escape so that he may once more satisfy his longing for a rendezvous in the secret haven.

Is this mysterious undertaking accomplished with wonderful gifts of rhapsody, flowers, music, candy, jewelry, cars, or houses? I do not know entirely. For some wives, one or all may do. All that matters is *your* wife and *her* desires. You'll have to ask the one who is the object of your affections, "What is romance to you?"

One evening after returning home from New Zealand, Bunny and I were attending the Christian Booksellers Association convention, and during our publisher's reception, I overheard the following conversation. Given the fact that the subject was more than just a little bit important to me, I eavesdropped.

One author was recently married, and was involved in small talk, which suddenly turned serious. This woman asked a key employee of the publishing company, "Why does romance have to die after marriage?"

With a puzzled look on his face, knowing very well the two people in question, he did not hesitate to remind her how he had personally witnessed the generous material expressions of affection lavished upon her by her husband.

Her response to him was, "That's not romance."

"It's not?" he responded. "Then what is romance?"

"Let me think about that for a moment," she replied. She walked a short distance away to contemplate the question.

As you may well imagine, I did not move. I waited for her return so I could hear her response. When she returned, she said, "Romance is knowing that you are still being pursued."

To me this spoke volumes. It was important to me for several reasons, but mostly because I was on a mission to know the answer for Bunny's sake.

If nothing else I have to say means anything worthwhile to you, I hope you can appreciate the value of this small deposit gleaned from a passing conversation. It certainly helped me.

Blessed

Wow! Do you have any idea how blessed I am to be married to a man who feels that way about romance? It's hard to believe that at one point in our marriage I felt Frank had no clue about how to romance me. One of my greatest joys is that he took the time to learn.

You would probably be surprised at how little effort it will take for you to romance your wife. Every woman is different; so don't get advice from another woman. Instead, research your wife. Study her as you would a new golf course you are about to play, or a project you're about to undertake at work. She will let you know exactly what to do. Listen for her "ooohs" and "aaahs" when she hears something romantic that another husband did for his wife. Listen, too, if she makes a comment while watching a movie. Ask her questions and give her multiple choice answers such as, "What speaks romance to you? 1) acts of service, 2) kind words, 3) thoughtfulness, 4) gifts, 5) affection." Let me suggest that you arrange that list in what you think is her order of priority, and see how well you know her. When she responds, ask her to be specific.

Romance most often comes in little ways. Think about your wife's past requests, and calculate just how much time it would take to complete the task. And don't be put off by practical requests, assuming they aren't "romantic." Has she ever asked you to bathe the children? Figure on 20–30 minutes, and if you do it with a willing heart, you will be blessed with the quality time you've spent with them.

Let me assure you, one of the greatest acts of romance is to offer to help with household responsibilities without waiting for her to ask. Taking out the trash costs you 3–5 minutes. And posing the question, "Do you need any help?" when you see her scurrying about doing endless tasks can have a profound impact in your secret haven. Many times she will probably say no, but your asking will mean so much to her. Go ahead, try it, and watch her pleased expression. I might add that its greatest impact comes when you do it regularly and complete the task in a timely manner.

I used to tell Frank that I see romance in the little things. One day I was getting a manicure, and as I was about to pay the manicurist she stopped me and said, "Oh no, Mrs. Wilson, your husband knew you were coming in today so he came by and paid for your manicure." I wish you could have seen the smile on my face! Now just how much time did it take Frank to do that kind deed? It was a small investment that paid high dividends in my heart.

Let me quickly add that I've discovered Frank likes to be romanced as well. One day I tried to guess how he likes to be romanced and assumed that it would somehow involve a home-cooked meal. When I inquired, however, his response was somewhat different: "Romance to me is knowing that when I've told you something, you've heard me, and you will follow through." That's romance? Well, it is to him. And since that day, I've worked hard in that area. I understand now that this relaxes him mentally and frees him up to pursue me.

Didn't you get married to have fun? Let's assume you thought you were marrying your best friend and that life would be filled with laughter, satisfaction, and good times. Is that what happened? In most cases the answer is no. Why? Usually it is because we did not apply God's principles for a successful marriage and we find ourselves reaping the consequences. We can blame our spouses, or we can take individual responsibility and today begin fixing what is broken. It will take time and consistency, but it is well worth the effort.

Combination Lock

Romance enhances physical intimacy. It's the oil that greases the wheel for a woman. But once things are in motion, it's important to know how to proceed.

I liken our bodies to a combination lock. No two bodies are the same, just as each leaf on a tree and every snowflake is unique. There are no two handprints or fingerprints the same. Doesn't it stand to reason that God would create every person's body different as well?

That is why our bodies are like combination locks. The only way one spouse can effectively open the other's lock is by discovering the correct sequence. In order to obtain it, a husband could spend a lifetime with his ear next to it, hoping to hear a click. He might even attempt to pry it open. However, the most beneficial and productive way for him to obtain the combination is for his wife to give it to him. And that probably means he has to ask.

What arouses and excites one person can be an utter turnoff for another. That is why having had sex with other people is a curse to a marriage. It provokes assumptions about what satisfies the spouse, and it also generates comparisons. Once again, God's forgiveness needs to be invoked (please do this in the privacy of your own heart. Nothing good will come of you sharing this with your wife). You'll also need to decide to drop all foregone conclusions about what your wife wants or needs. The two of you should effectively and sensitively share with each other your sexual combinations.

A woman once said to me, "Oh, I could never do that. I'm too shy!" My response was, "You can do it. Just play the hot-and-cold game. If he kisses or touches you in one place and there is no feeling in that area then say, 'Cold, cold!' Maybe the next place will be 'Warm, warm.' But what you're looking for is 'Hot, hot, HOT!'"

Over time your wife will acquire your various combinations as well. She will know what to do and say when you are happy, sad, discouraged, or tired. As these lessons are learned, the secret haven becomes an even more irresistible oasis for release, rest, and relaxation.

Sometimes a woman comes to me and inquires about what to do if her husband wants to have sex every day. It's too often for her, and the husband refuses to change. Worse yet, he gets angry when she wants to talk about it. Once again, I want to turn this portion over to Frank because if you're that husband, I'd like you to get a man's response.

Frank's Insights

The key word for a Christian in any activity is *moderation*. Everything that exceeds moderation has great potential for bondage. Philippians 4:5 says, "Let your moderation be known unto all men. The Lord is at hand" (KJV).

What about the conduct of sexual relations between a man and his wife? Can the quality of moderation apply to that? Absolutely. That is why I encourage both the man and his wife to fully enjoy one another as they grow into maturity. One thing, and one thing alone should govern sex, and that is *agape* love. *Agape* love seeks the highest good of the one who is the object of your affections. It is patient, kind, and is not self-seeking. In the eyes of love, the object is always the recipient of the lover's full and unselfish attention.

Strangely, nowhere in Scripture does God command the woman to love her husband. But in several places throughout Scripture, he says to the man, "Love your wife, cheer her up, and honor her." I do not believe the Lord would have commanded men along this course without also providing them with the strength and wisdom they need to accomplish the task.

There is a great parallel between what God expects of a husband toward his beloved, and what He Himself has done for His bride-to-be. Therefore, if a husband is so controlled by his physiological urges he cannot practice loving his wife like Christ loved the church, he has a spiritual problem that needs to be addressed. Once he solves that, he will solve the sexual issue as well.

Love is more concerned about caring for the object of its desire than having its own needs met. Consequently, sex practiced according to the biblical description of love (1 Corinthians 13), and in obedience to it, will be mutually gratifying. It will have to be so, in order for it to be approved by God.

If a wife has emotional pain and is under mental duress, her needs are more important than her husband's longing for sexual satisfaction. Because the husband loves his wife, he will place his own desires on the back burner. God will provide the strength necessary for him to govern himself and turn his attention toward ministering to the concerns of his wife.

By this time, I know you are wondering, *What about* my *sexual needs? What about her loving* me *and seeing* my *highest good?* If you think you need sex three times a day, and your wife is giving in to your addiction, that doesn't necessarily mean that she is seeking your greatest well-being. Christian counseling is a must for cracking this juggernaut.

On the other hand, Christian counseling is also my recommendation if you desire sex on a reasonable basis, and your request continues to be unmet.

Of course, there is the possibility that it is the wife, not the husband, who is reading this chapter because curiosity got the best of her. If so, and if your husband wants sex on a daily basis, and you are at a loss as to what to do, my advice is to be patient. God is at work, and perhaps the best solution is not for you to give this chapter to your husband.

Have you noticed that he is resistant to your teaching him? I'm sure you have. Instead of trying to instruct him, read and apply to yourself the information written in this book. In chapter 9, Bunny shares on how to resolve issues, and that applies to this situation as well. What's most important is that you have a healthy outlook towards sex.

Husbands, let's return to what I believe is really the heart of the matter of romance and intimacy.

I once heard Pastor Haman Cross say, "If you want a blaze in the bedroom, you have to start a fire in the kitchen." The principle here is clear. We reap what we sow. To start a fire, we must strike a match. Therefore, romance and sex go hand in hand. Bunny intimated the same thought earlier in this chapter when she talked about the small things men can do in romancing their mates. If you want your wife to respond enthusiastically, you must take the time to do the little things that cause her to warm up and purr before you try to put things into gear and take off. This requires four things: planning, timing, time, and tenderness.

I suppose it is only natural for youngsters who are growing into adulthood to be impatient and self-serving. And yet for me, knowing that did not alleviate the frustration I felt each time I allowed one of our teenagers to use the car. Why? It was because of my inability to convince them it was important to let the automobile warm up before they put it into gear. I could not for the life of me figure out why this was so complicated for them. Not, that is, until I remembered their age and anxious state of mind. Once I got them to check out the owner's operational manual, it was easier to reason with them and to convince them about the necessity of proper care for the long-term health of an automobile.

But what about the mature man? Let's take a look at this same scenario from the perspective of intimate relations by considering the four things necessary for romance:

Planning. With the exception of spontaneous sexual combustion, i.e., two people on fire and raring to go, a married man usually knows beforehand that he desires sex right now and will most certainly want to have it later on that evening. However, he seldom makes plans to accomplish this goal. He just hops in the sack, sometimes omitting a shower or bath, and expects it to happen automatically, without proper preparation, mentally or romantically. That is like getting into that automobile first thing in the morning and taking off without warming it up. You will eventually ruin the engine or, as in this case, your wife's sexual desire.

Timing. Before you start making your moves, you need to answer a question or two. What kind of day has she had? How is she feeling? What can you do to upgrade her excitement for making love without degrading its beauty? Be certain your actions show you care more for her concerns than for your desires.

Time. Here are a few things that will help her mentally prepare for love, that is, if she is not already there.

- Instead of expecting her to prepare the evening meal, you do so, or take her out for dinner.

- If you stay home instead, help clear the table, and stack the dishes in the sink or dishwasher.

- Prepare for her a nice hot bath, or help the children with their homework.

Tenderness. Intimacy is to see into me. It is something that we all desire, but women are apt to appreciate it more than men. In many instances, its importance to her is greater than the pleasure of sex itself. The goal of intimacy is for her to know you, and for you to know what is on her mind and in her heart. She wants to tell you how she feels, but she needs to be sure you are listening. Therefore, intimacy requires a tender heart and a sensitive spirit that does not list sex as the crowning achievement of your time in the secret haven.

In a word, if romance were a stamp, sex would be the letter, and the price of the stamp would determine how far the letter travels. If romance were the invitation, sex would be the dance. So if there is no invitation, there may not be a dance.

An extreme situation (a husband desiring sex three times a day regularly), represents the addictions of the old nature. We need to break our bondage to those addictions before they break us. We can become their slaves, or allow the Lord to become their Master. The odds for gaining complete control over them without the supernatural intervention of God are very low.

Addictions begin in the thought life and slowly work their way into our souls. The word of God teaches us how to resist the demands of our carnal nature and control it.

Someone may ask, "But what about the natural biological urges of the flesh?"

Have you ever known some people who eat all the time? Their appetite hardly ever seems satisfied. If they do not get a handle on it, they may wind up in a hospital or worse still, dead of a stroke. At the very least, they don't look very attractive.

Likewise, a sexual appetite that is out of control carries at least an equal if not a greater potential for physical, emotional, and psychological damage to you and your spouse.

The addicted husband (or wife) is hanging by a thread spiritually, even though he or she may not know it.

The plain point is this: *Our addictions can become our testimony or our tomb.* The choice is up to us. With the help of the Lord, we can overcome them. The affected spouse must start now breaking the patterns of addictions in his/her life before they become permanently ingrained characteristics that are emotionally crippling.

The Hard Stuff

Thank you, Frank, for your wisdom and for being the kind of husband who edifies me as a wife. I could not have written this book without your blessing and guidance. You have inspired me to become the woman God created me to be in this world.

Gentlemen, how much do you want to enhance your marriage and secret haven? If this is what you really desire, will you allow me to share some difficult principles that may be hard for you to read? Perhaps the following information does not apply to you at all, but I think you'll find it valuable to know why the things I'm about to mention are a hindrance to a satisfying sexual experience. You may find yourself needing to advise your son, nephew, or a male friend about the pitfalls of these debilitating habits.

I talked at great length earlier in this book about pornography, masturbation, and fantasy. Suffice it to say that if you are or have been a participant in any or all of them, it is almost assured that your sex life is suffering. You've been "robbed blind," and that was the exact intent of the culprit, Satan, who longs to keep you shielded from the truth. The violation is so great that it can devastate the pleasure God created for a husband and wife.

"In the last days, men [and women] will be lovers of themselves" (2 Timothy 3:2). Their focus is self-satisfaction, and the fantasy figures that live in their imagination have no flaws. These mental sex objects never say anything hurtful, they are always sensitive to needs, and they don't have bad breath! Who can compete with that vision? Reality can never match fantasy, because fantasy seems perfect.

Masturbation allows people to satisfy themselves, and once that is mastered, there is little chance that a spouse can duplicate the exact touch and pressure required to bring about the same result. A good number of those who masturbate prior to marriage continue the practice after marriage. God never intended for us to discover ourselves—that pleasure was reserved for our spouse.

It has been taught in certain circles that masturbation is not a violation because it does not involve anyone else. But as Christians, we are never alone. God is watching, Jesus is praying for us, and the Holy Spirit lives inside us. Masturbation forces the Holy Spirit to participate. It corrodes the heart, soul, and mind.

Deuteronomy 6:5 says, "Love the LORD your God with *all* your heart and with *all* your soul and with *all* your strength" (emphasis added). Simply stated, the heart represents that place where we make our decisions. The soul is our emotions and the mind is where we think our thoughts. The word *all* signifies everything in every way.

What do people think about when they masturbate? Are their thoughts pure and holy? Could they perform the act while praying? If your answer is yes, then the deception in your life is so great it will take a miracle for you to break free. During the act of masturbation, people's thoughts follow along a certain path. Perhaps they focus on a pornographic picture, where they imagine themselves with a stranger. Or they may choose a more flowery scene

*D*id a loving parent with a good healthy attitude toward the subject sit down with you and paint a beautiful picture of what you would enjoy once you were married?

that involves a romantic interlude with someone they know, consummating their passionate display of lust.

A person who masturbates can fantasize about being with anyone at any time. In his or her mind, partners can change as often as they want to, and nobody gets hurt. No one needs to know except them.

If you are involved in pornography and masturbation (they go hand in hand—pun intended), you'll have to make the decision that they are wrong, and then turn away. The rose-colored glasses you're wearing will have to be removed and replaced with a new set of lenses. It's time for you to see things as God sees them.

Suppose you are very hungry, and a beautifully decorated table is wheeled in and placed in front of you. Your favorite plate of food is under a silver dome, waiting for the waiter to remove it. Putting your napkin in your lap and picking up your knife and fork, you watch in anxious anticipation. When the cover is removed, it is indeed your favorite meal, but it is crawling with white squirming maggots. Will you still eat the meal? No, I don't think so. Suddenly you no longer have an appetite.

When you see pornography and masturbation through God's eyes, you will turn away in disgust. Even though they may have been among your favorite activities, you will no longer want to be associated with them. You realize that they are a lie, and that you were never alone. Your fantasy is crawling with maggots of deception, selfishness, and lust.

When you come face-to-face with the sins of pornography and masturbation, God requires you to have a repentant heart. To repent means that you acknowledge your sin and turn and go another way. King David handled his sins by saying, "I have considered my ways and have turned my steps to your statutes" (Psalm 119:59).

Our addictions can become our testimony or our tomb.

Jesus was tempted as we are tempted, and He had the same feelings as the rest of us. What did He do with them? He exercised self-control, and so can you. He is our example of purity and holiness. Philippians 4:13 reminds us, "I can do all things through Christ who strengthens me" (NKJV). First Peter 1:14-15 encourages, "As obedient children, not conforming yourselves to the former lusts, as in your ignorance; but as He who called you is holy, you also be holy in all your conduct" (NKJV).

Not only do you need to turn away from pornography and masturbation, you also need to turn toward your wife. No, she is not the perfect person lodged in your fantasy. Like you, she has flaws, but God will help you to love her, imperfections and all.

You are now in a position to direct your heart to the secret haven. There you will uncover wonderful experiences difficult to imagine because you are there with a real tridimensional person—one who is body, soul, and spirit. The dynamics continually shift, and intimate discoveries can always be made. Every encounter in the secret place is somewhat different because as human beings we are continually changing. Can you see how that adds to the excitement?

The Real World

Are you in a difficult marriage? Every marriage has its set of challenges, but in most cases, they can be repaired with the proper application of God's principles. I often say, "There is no way to judge the condition of your marriage until you do it God's way." And that takes more than one application. It means we do and say the right things over and over again.

In your eyes, your wife may have become the most unappealing person in the world. That means you need to find a new perspective from which to view her. If you have been addicted to pornography and/or masturbation, she may have changed because of her constant frustration with and rejection of your behavior.

What if your wife doesn't know the Lord and couldn't care less about the secret haven? Suppose she is insensitive to your sexual needs and desires. Was she uncaring when you married her? What signs did you see while you were dating her? Even though you may not have had sex before marriage, did you discuss it? What did she lead you to believe?

> *E*very encounter in the secret haven is somewhat different because as human beings we are continually changing.

It's important to accept responsibility for how we conducted our dating and courting activities. Many mistakes are made during that season, and the consequences are long-range. But be encouraged—we serve a healing God who wants to help you with every aspect of your marriage.

What if illness prohibits one of you from participating in sex? Are you impotent? Don't despair—this condition is often reversible with the proper medical attention and counseling. What if the wife is menopausal and experiencing changes in her body that make sex uncomfortable for her? What if you suspect or have discovered that she is committing adultery? Even in the difficult cases, there are answers if you are willing to search them out. James 1:5-8 teaches us:

> If any of you lacks wisdom, he should ask God, who gives generously to all without finding fault, and it will be given to him. But when he asks, he must believe and not doubt, because he who doubts is like a wave of the sea, blown and tossed by the wind. That man should not think he will receive anything from the Lord; he is a double-minded man, unstable in all he does.

Sometimes our lives feel as if Satan has planted emotional and mental land mines all around us, and they explode when we remember or recall painful past experiences. This will affect your enjoyment in the secret haven. Perhaps your father or mother rejected you, or a schoolteacher made you feel stupid. Maybe on your job you feel inadequate or incompetent. Then there is that friend who stabbed you in the back. Many are the challenges of life, and how we respond to each one affects our secret haven. Is there unforgivingness and resentment in your heart toward people who have hurt you? That person may very well be your spouse.

Forgiveness is essential in the secret haven. A simple definition of forgiveness is to give up your right to judge offenders, and to release them to God. After all, isn't that what Jesus did for us? The Lord's Prayer says, "Forgive us our debts *as* we forgive our debtors." One of the greatest gifts we can give ourselves is to release those who have hurt us. It frees us up to love again.

We also need to beware of worry and anxiety. Both are sins that lead to frustration and rob us of pleasure in the secret haven. Jesus teaches in Matthew 6:25–27, "Therefore I tell you, do not worry about your life....Who of you by worrying can add a single hour to his life?" And 1 Peter 5:7 says you should, "cast all your anxiety upon him because he cares for you."

Fear, doubt, self-pity, and anger are also sins that need to be dealt with in our lives. Chapters 3 and 5 in this book may give aid and comfort to you. We can be free of the bondages that bind us and can learn to walk in the glorious freedom God has for each of His children.

Exciting, dynamic sex between you and your wife is God's intention for your secret haven. When that is missing, it is your responsibility as the head of the household to obtain the wisdom to correct the problem. It is a journey you have to be willing to make no matter how long it takes. The rewards are great, and the effort is well worthwhile.

Wrapping It Up

I appreciate Frank taking the time to share with you husbands. One of the things I am most grateful for is that my husband doesn't allow his past to determine his present actions. The fact that he never heard his father tell his mother that he loved her does not stop him from being verbally and physically affectionate toward me.

Frank's father was a lecturer, and Frank was, also, when I married him. When he became irritated about something, he would talk on and on and on. But he allowed the Word of God to change him, and he no longer communicates that way. There are a number of areas in which he has changed, and I know it hasn't been easy for him. Above all else, Frank Wilson is committed to not breaking God's heart with his words and actions.

Likewise, let me encourage you husbands to apply God's principles to your marriage. Set your sights long range and don't let temporary disappointments discourage you. Your wife longs to be accepted, appreciated, and approved. She wants to be romanced, and she wants you to be the only one on earth who knows how to romance her. She is a gift from the Lord longing to be opened. Discovering new, godly ways to do this will profoundly affect your relationship and will greatly enhance your pleasures in the secret haven.

Before We Begin:
A Word to the Parent
or Guardian

~

Young people are dear to my heart. If we think growing up was difficult when we were kids, we need to double our compassion for today's youth and what they face. There are suggestions of illicit sex everywhere: on the front covers of magazines at market checkout stands, on prime-time television (even the commercials), on videos, and on the Internet. And, unfortunately, the sexual escapades of a former president that appeared on the front pages of our newspapers for months only added to their dilemma.

Our teenagers don't have to look for sex. A quick sensual image can flash before their eyes at any moment. As adults, we not only need to understand God's design for sexuality, we must also equip Christian youth to stand in God's truth so they can make a conscious and knowledgeable decision to abstain until they marry.

When I consider the negative attitudes and poor examples that prevail among many adult believers about sex, I can't help but wonder why we should expect our teenagers to wait until they get married. What incentives do we give them to remain sexually pure? Even while they try to stay strong in their decision not to participate, some of their classmates arrive at school applauding the sexual escapades they had the night before. Do our children have a firm foundation underlying their decision not to join in the sexual experimentation of their peers?

If they choose to abstain, what is their reason for abstaining? For some it's fear—the fear of getting pregnant, contracting a sexually transmitted disease, or disappointing their parents. Still others wait because they have been taught that premarital sex is a sin against God. But is that enough to keep their raging desires under control? Just how many times do we all sin against God or disappoint Him in every other way? Why should premarital sex be any different? Why not just have some fun and trust God to forgive and forget later on?

No, our children need a solid reason to keep themselves sexually pure. They need reinforcement so exciting that it forces them to make the conscious decision to abstain from self-gratification through sex, masturbation, and pornography. They need a belief so true and powerful that it can support them during times of great temptation. That truth can be embodied in the statement, *Don't settle for anything less than saved sex!*

Saved sex is discussed at great length in this book, and if you are planning to take an interactive role while your teenager reads the following chapter, I hope you'll read the rest of the book yourself. Following is a list of suggested questions that can stimulate conversation with your teenager about sex:

1. Do you ever hear comments concerning sex that are confusing?

2. When you have questions, where do you look for answers?

3. Are you familiar with the term *saved sex?*

4. Do you know why it's important to wait until you're married to experience physical intimacy? Explain.

5. What should you say to someone of the opposite sex if they said to you, "If you love me, you would...(have sex)?"

The above questions are intended to be icebreakers. This book is full of answers to give teens about their sexuality, and it provides numerous reasons to abstain. Our teenagers need a confidante who will give them sound reasons for celibacy, and that confidante must be rooted and grounded in a healthy understanding of God's intentions for sex. If you are involved in the life of a teen, maybe God is calling you to be that kind of a godly friend. If so, I hope you'll read this book including the pages that follow, allow your teenager to read the following chapter, and then talk about it together.

> Warning: The following material may be too mature for some teenagers. Parental discretion is advised.

11

To the Point (for Teenagers Only)

~

You may be surprised that this chapter was given to you. You may even feel a little embarrassed if you already know what it is about. Almost every teenager has some unanswered concerns regarding sex. Are there things you've questioned and have found difficult to talk to anyone about? If so, there is a good chance I will address some of those things in the following pages.

There is very little information written on the subject of sex for teenagers from a Christian point of view, and that is why I wrote this chapter for you. Even if you feel uncomfortable talking about sex, I encourage you to continue reading because there may be some information that will be helpful to you.

Confused

When my older children were teenagers, they learned about the different parts of their body in school during health class, even though the class did not actually include specific lessons about sexual activity. The school didn't give any details in that area, and I was too ashamed to talk about it. You see, my parents didn't teach me anything like that, and so when I became a mother of teenagers, I understood why they didn't share their feelings with me about this sensitive subject. Imagine for a moment that you are a parent (be serious now) and your teenage son or daughter is sitting across from you. She or he wants you to answer some questions about sex. What would you say? If you think about it, you'll agree that it's a challenging subject.

One day I decided to begin looking through the Bible to find out what God's Word had to say on the topic, and it was there that I found the truth. Then whenever one of my children brought the subject up, I knew what to tell them. For example, I remember the day when I was sitting cross-legged on the bed playing a board game with one of my younger daughters, who was nine years old at the time. She searched her letters and then shouted, "I have a word!" Her smile, however, quickly turned to a look of distress and she hastily added, "No, I don't."

"Let me see," I said.

She responded, "No, it's okay. I'll find another."

"Come on," I nudged.

"You'll get mad."

"No, I won't."

Slowly, she turned her letters around and, with flushed cheeks, she revealed the source of her embarrassment. With three little letters she made it clear it was time for me to set her foundation on how she viewed the subject of *s-e-x*. Obviously she was beginning to hear comments and opinions from her schoolmates. It was my responsibility to teach her the truth. There would be time for me to say more, but at that moment what was called for was an appropriate response.

She searched my face for a reaction and I announced, "That's a good word! Sex was created by God, and that makes it wonderful."

This sensitive child seemed to sigh with relief as we returned to our game. Gone was the concerned expression, and it was now replaced with a smile. I stored that moment away in my heart, knowing it was just the first baby step that we would take together on her path to womanhood.

You may have just become a teenager and are not yet spending much time wondering about sex. You can, however, see the changes taking place within your body. Whenever you see a couple kiss or express affection, there may be an unusual stirring within you that you never really noticed before. That is the beginning of sexual desire, and God created those feelings. It is a normal sensation, but it must be controlled until after you are married.

You may have reached the age where you are attracted to someone of the opposite sex, and you're not sure how far to go and how far not to go in a relationship. Is holding hands a good idea? Is it okay to kiss? What about hugging each other affectionately? You may also be sorting through a number of different sources, comments, and opinions by friends or fellow students on the subject of sex. Thankfully, there is no reason for you to wonder about the truth when God took the time to write it in the Bible.

> *A*lmost every teenager I know has some unanswered questions concerning sex.

The Truth

My daughter Christy chose to attend a university in New York City. As a freshman, she was excited about the dormitory experience. One day she called home and said, "Mom, I was walking down the hallway of my dorm, and you'll never guess what I saw. Someone hung a poster on the door that says, 'It's not premarital sex if you don't plan to get married!'"

Christy laughed and continued, "At first I thought about how much sense that made, but as I kept walking I thought, *Hey, wait a minute. That's wrong!* Mom, it seemed to be such a logical statement, and if a Christian person doesn't know the Bible and the truth about sex, I can see how easily they could be misled by such a cunning lie."

The truth is God wants you to wait until you're married to have sex. And no, He is not trying to punish you. Instead, He wants to bless you. Have you made the decision to wait until after marriage to have sex? What is your reason? Is it fear—the fear of getting pregnant, contracting a sexually transmitted disease, or disappointing your parents?

Or is it because you've been taught that sexual involvement before marriage is a sin against God? That will usually keep you strong until you meet the person you believe you're going to marry one day. That's when sexual temptation can get really strong. After all, you do plan to get married one day anyway, right? The devil will whisper, "Why wait?" He may try to convince you that even though sex is a sin, people sin against God or disappoint Him every day in other ways. So why should premarital sex—having sex before marriage—be any different? Why not just have some fun and trust God to forgive and forget later on?

You need a solid reason to keep yourself sexually pure—a belief so true and powerful that it can hold you during times of great temptation. That truth can be embodied in the statement *Don't settle for anything less than saved sex!*

Saved sex is more rewarding than anything the world has to offer and can only be enjoyed by a man and woman who have been joined together by God in holy matrimony. Sex is the only action in the Bible that is sinful when you are single and holy when you are married. It is an act blessed by

God Himself. So precious is the experience that you'll be robbed blind if you participate in unsaved sex prior to your wedding night.

Sex is a celebration of God's creation, and He is pleased when we fulfill our desire in marriage. Since God designed it, doesn't it stand to reason He would be happy when we operate according to His plan? Participating in sex as God conceived it results in satisfaction for both partners. To violate the principle of saved sex is a lonely and unfulfilling experience. It subtracts God from the equation and leads to a desolate place. Each encounter lessens the possibility that true satisfaction will ever be found.

An understanding of saved sex begins with the awareness that sexuality is God's creation. In the book of Genesis, it was God who brought Adam and Eve together. The Lord made the man and shaped the woman. He then presented Eve to Adam, and boy, was he glad! It's important to note that Genesis 2:25 says, "The man and his wife were both naked and they felt no shame." The first couple was free to see each other in their deepest, most intimate selves without embarrassment, guilt, or fear.

Sin caused Adam and Eve to feel shame, cover their bodies, and try to hide their faces from God. From that day forward, sex became something to be hidden and revealed only in the dark places of a room or in our minds. Sex became the devil's workshop, where distortion was created and lies were born. "Stolen water is sweet," (Proverbs 9:17) became the devil's theme song. I believe it's time for us to write our own songs, and not be "conformed to this world, but be transformed by the renewing of your mind" (Romans 12:2 NKJV).

The concept of saved sex prepares you to live a life that is wholly and completely devoted to God. It strengthens your ability to wait until God blesses you with the mate He has chosen for you. Coming into the knowledge of how

> *Don't settle for anything less than saved sex!*

saved sex works will increase your desire to experience nothing less than God's best for you, and that is saved sex. You will see sexual temptations through a new set of eyes, and situations which at one time would have stimulated you to fall into sin now seem distasteful from the very beginning. Understanding saved sex before marriage prepares you for a fulfilling sex life after marriage.

Consequences of Unsaved Sex

I knew society would be trying to instruct my daughter Christy on the subject of sex, so I chose to put my thoughts on paper one day and urged her to consider the consequences of premarital sex. The list is as follows:

1. It will break God's heart.

2. Sin will enter the relationship and negatively change it.

3. A loss of respect from the boy toward the girl (usually unspoken), no matter what he tells you.

4. God created man to be the pursuer. Once you have been conquered, an element of fun and excitement leaves the relationship.

5. You'll lose your "specialness" (even though he'll swear differently).

6. There will be nothing to look forward to on your wedding night.

7. Once you begin, what will be your reason for stopping? Use that reason now.

8. It will come to be expected.

9. Possible pregnancy.

10. Guilt will enter the relationship.

11. Your self-control will be destroyed. You will need this in your marriage to ward off other sins, including adultery.

12. Your Christian testimony will be tainted.

13. Your younger sister is following in your footsteps. Is this what you would want for her?

14. You'll lose your testimony with your children. What will you tell them when they reach their teenage years and ask you what you did when you were young?

15. You'll weaken your potential husband's walk in Christ, and he will be your spiritual leader one day.

That list of consequences is thought-provoking. But maybe you're thinking, "Help! It's too late." If you are a teenager who has already participated in sex, is everything lost? No, it is not. That is why it is so exciting to serve a forgiving God. The best decision is to abstain (not have sex before marriage), but if you have already had sex, then God is calling you to repent of the sin of fornication and make the commitment to wait until after you are married to have another sexual experience. That decision is called celibacy. The goal is to remain *celibate* so you can one day *celebrate* your sexuality with your spouse.

Once you repent and decide to settle for nothing less than saved sex, you will notice how differently you feel when you are placed in the kind of tempting situations you have faced before.

Perhaps a boy or girl you're interested in begins to make sexual comments to you, such as, "I wish we could be alone so I could discover your hidden secrets." In the past you might have smiled and nodded. But now that you know the truth about saved sex, your response will probably be much different. You're insulted that he or she would suggest such a thing. It soils the relationship. Besides, since that is what he or she is after, perhaps it would be best for you to find someone else to spend your time with, someone who believes as you do.

> *The* goal is to remain *celibate* so you can one day *celebrate* your sexuality with your spouse.

There is a lot of misinformation going around about sex. You can get your knowledge from God's school or the world's school. You don't actually *attend* the world's school, but it's message comes to you in bits and pieces. One lesson may come over the radio, on a CD, or the computer. Another may appear through suggestive pictures on TV, movies, or video. But let's imagine for a minute that all the information is housed in one place. What would it look like?

The World's School

"Greetings. Come right in to the Modern World's Academy of Sexual Pleasure. Teenagers, you are welcome. My name is Dr. D. There is room for everyone, but please be patient while standing in the long lines. As you make your way to the front door, notice that we've gone to great lengths to beautify the building. Isn't the landscaping fabulous? A great deal of thought went into constructing something that would be functional yet pleasing to your eye."

With hopes high and fantasy receivers intact, prospective students wait eagerly to enroll to learn all they can. As they read through the list of courses offered and study the class descriptions, their hearts pound with excitement about all they will be learning. The list goes on and on but following are a few highlights:

- It's your body and you can do whatever you like with it as long as you're not hurting anyone.

- Sex is designed to satisfy an individual personally, and how that is accomplished is each person's choice.

- Having sex before marriage won't affect you after you are married.

- There is nothing wrong with satisfying yourself; the act of masturbation* eliminates unwanted pregnancies, relieves stress, and brings a sweet release.

- If you are a female participant, should you conceive during sex, then abortion is a viable solution.

- Teenage boys, you are free to "sow your wild oats" so you can get your sex drive out of your system and settle down later.

There is certainly another way of looking at sexuality, but you won't find it in the Modern World's Academy of Sexual Pleasure. Mr. D (short for Deception) tricks us into believing something is true when in fact it is false. The world's school teaches sex without shame but neglects to mention that guilt is a required subject. And nobody talks about the deep regret that follows each participant down the halls of time. Wisdom is not part of the curriculum, and sexual freedom becomes one huge playground.

One of the lessons the world's school will try to teach you is that sexual self-gratification—also called masturbation*—is just fine and is, in fact, a healthy way to deal with desire. The world also promotes the use of sexually stimulating images, which are called pornography. Many times these two work together. It is important for you to know that they are both inappropriate for Christians and can lead you away from God and His best for you.

---

* Masturbation is self-gratification. It is when a person explores their own genital area with the intent of satisfying their sexual desire.

Pornography and masturbation are addictive, and are not part of God's plan for saved sex. Proverbs 23:7 says, "As he thinks in his heart, so is he" (NKJV). It is essential for us to keep our thoughts pure and to keep our minds free from enticing and impure images. That means avoiding some magazines, movies, and books and not getting involved in certain Internet chat rooms. These are danger zones for teenagers.

> *The world's school teaches sex without shame but neglects to mention that guilt is a required subject.*

And here's a word to the wise: If you struggle with attractions to people of your same sex, or if you have been exposed to sexuality in an inappropriate way because someone touched you or otherwise violated your body, *please talk to a responsible Christian adult about it.* A pastor or a godly relative will help you if you cannot talk to your parents. And please don't feel you have to protect the person who misused you—if you do, she or he will continue to violate others.

How Far Is Too Far?

Once you've made the decision to wait for saved sex, you're still going to have some questions about what is appropriate between boys and girls and what isn't. For example, are there any consequences to kissing and hugging? Yes, there are. Physical contact ignites sexual desire. In most cases, sex begins with a kiss. It is the starting place, and once the flame of sexual desire is lit, it is extremely difficult to control. It is easier for a girl to "turn it off" than it is for a boy, but nobody is immune to temptation.

By now, you have probably learned that the boy has a chemical in his body called *testosterone*. Girls have it in small quantities, but boys have it in abundance! When testosterone enters a young man's bloodstream, he becomes sexually aroused, and this causes him to have a physical reaction in his body. Kissing intensifies this reaction, and it become very uncomfortable for him. He will probably want more than a kiss, and before long a girl may want more, too.

If you are a boy, what are you supposed to do when testosterone enters your bloodstream (usually every 72 hours) and you are sexually aroused? It is important to know that testosterone can be used for more than satisfying your sexual desires. It is a creative agent that should be channeled into other areas before marriage. Applying yourself mentally to your studies and physically to work and sports helps to release the pressure from testosterone. If handled correctly, you will probably be the smartest and strongest boy in your school. But controlling your thought life and physical contact with the opposite sex is a must.

Young ladies, it is your responsibility to do all you can to help a Christian brother stay pure before marriage. I believe one of the reasons God gave boys testosterone is to propel them into doing great things. When channeled properly, it is quite a motivating force. It will also make a young man a great husband, once he's married.

How can God use you to keep a young man on track? Please, keep your conversation and behavior clean. What you say and how you dress can have a positive or negative effect on him. Do your best not to stimulate his sexual desire. You can do that in a number of ways.

Because today's fashions are so revealing, you must watch what you wear. Don't fall into the trap of needing attention so badly that you dress provocatively. I once heard a man say, "If it ain't for sale, take down the sign!" That doesn't mean you can't be fashionable, it means that you are sensitive about not accentuating your body parts for the purpose of stimulating a young man's desire.

Some girls might say, "If he's sexually aroused by the way I dress, then that is his problem, not mine." Not so. Philippians 2:3-4 says, "Do nothing out of selfish ambition or vain conceit, but in humility consider others better than yourselves. Each of you should look not only to your own interests, but also to the interests of others."

God would love to use you as His representative to live a clean and wholesome life for Him and to set an example for others. A young man who wants to serve God will be attracted to your purity.

And what about your sex drive? Since you have low levels of testosterone, does that mean you also have low sexual desire? Absolutely not. A girl's sexual desire can be just as great or greater than a boy's, depending on her chemistry and thought life. The mind can be a tremendous sexual stimulant. As I said before, you must guard against sensual material both visually or mentally.

Also, there are two to three days in the month when you are ovulating (during which eggs pass from one of your ovaries into your uterus). This usually happens about two weeks before your period. It is at this time that your body can get strong sexual desires because it wants to make a baby. My recommendation is that you take note of that fact and during that time, don't go out on a date—especially one-on-one.

What about oral sex? A newspaper recently reported that teenage pregnancy was down because oral sex was on the rise. That lets me know that this is a subject that must be addressed. Oral sex takes place when the mouth is placed on another person's genital area for the purpose of bringing sexual satisfaction. If anyone tells you this is not really sex, that is a lie. Oral sex accomplishes the same thing as intercourse, only with a different method. God wants you to abstain and remain pure.

Your Guarantee

If you are an older teenager with a steady boyfriend or girlfriend, you may be asking, "If I don't 'try it out' before marriage, how will I know whether the person I want to marry will be able to sexually satisfy me?" What is your guarantee?

Premarital counseling is essential to marital success, and when it comes to the subject of sex, it needs to include a male and female counselor. A male counselor must ask the young man (in private) if he is physically capable of meeting your sexual needs. A woman counselor should ask the female the same questions. If there is a problem, it must be discussed *before* marriage

> *Some girls might say, "If he's sexually aroused by the way I dress, then that is his problem, not mine."*

Once all that is out of the way and the marriage takes place, you are free to enjoy what God created for your pleasure. Remember, it will take a lifetime to discover what the Lord has reserved sexually for the husband and the wife.

God has truly saved the best for last. If you are willing to keep yourself free from sexual contact and activity prior to marriage, you will be able to one day look deeply into the eyes of your new husband or wife and utter three little words: "At last! Hallelujah!"

Other Books by P.B. Wilson and Frank Wilson

KNIGHT IN SHINING ARMOR
by *P.B. Wilson*
A million-and-a-half women will marry for the first time this year. But many others will become mired in a holding pattern waiting for their expectant marriages to take flight. This book breaks the holding pattern, showing women what to do while they wait, how to become complete in Christ as a single, and what to look for in a life partner.

LIBERATED THROUGH SUBMISSION
by *P.B. Wilson*
If you think this book is just for married women, you're in for a surprise. Submission, as it turns out, is for everyone, and destroys anger and rebellion while setting people free to love and give.

SEVEN SECRETS WOMEN WANT TO KNOW
by *P.B. Wilson*
"Giving God full reign over our lives releases us to reach our purpose and destiny." Using personal examples and thought-provoking illustrations, Bunny Wilson introduces women to the "S" factor—seven keys to overcoming discouragement, confusion, and frustration while soaring to new heights of joy and fulfillment.

MASTER'S DEGREE
by *Frank and P.B. Wilson*
This book explores the spiritual, emotional, and physical aspects of marriage, then shows how God views, supports, and participates in every relationship. Includes special sections for husbands only and for wives only.